Table of Contents

Practice Test #1

Practice Questions

1. Babies typically imitate various adult speech sounds around which ages?
   a. Birth to 3 months
   b. 4 to 6 months
   c. 7 months to 1 year
   d. 1 year to 18 months

2. It is developmentally normal for a child 8 to 12 months old to wave bye-bye. Which norm is this an example for?
   a. Pragmatics
   b. Semantics
   c. Phonology
   d. Syntax

3. A 1-year-old typically can point using the forefinger. What is this MOST closely associated with?
   a. Cognitive skills
   b. Motor skills
   c. Sensory skills
   d. Language skills

4. Primarily, what is the basic structure of the English language?
   a. Isolating or analytic
   b. Agglutinating or synthetic
   c. Amalgamating or polysynthetic
   d. Inflectional or fusional

5. Which of these concern(s) the patterns, systems, and rules of speech sounds in a language?
   a. Phonology
   b. Phonetics
   c. Phonemics
   d. All of these

6. Which of these ideas do the Universalist-Linguistic school of phonological acquisition theories include?
   a. Children develop phonological principles in a manner that is not linear.
   b. Children develop their phonological concepts through passive learning.
   c. Children demonstrate individual differences in phonological acquisition.
   d. Children demonstrate their phonological acquisition as active learners.

7. "By next week, we *will have completed* all four reports." The italicized part of the previous sentence is an example of which grammatical category?
   a. Person
   b. Case
   c. Tense
   d. Number

8. Parents say the word *bottle* every time they give their baby a bottle. In time, the baby responds the same way to hearing the word *bottle* alone without the actual bottle. In terms of behavioral learning theories of language development, what is this an example of?
   a. Classical conditioning
   b. Operant conditioning
   c. Social learning theory
   d. Constructivism theory

9. Models of behavior modification typically use which of the following to effect changes?
   a. What the individual is thinking
   b. What the individual is sensing
   c. What the individual is feeling
   d. What the individual is doing

10. Of the following theories of cognitive development, whose posits discrete developmental stages?
   a. Skinner's
   b. Vygotsky's
   c. Bandura's
   d. Piaget's

11. Among theories of language acquisition, which idea is MOST compatible with the observation that children develop language in similar patterns across various cultural contexts?
   a. B. F. Skinner's environmental influence
   b. Whorf's linguistic relativity hypothesis
   c. Noam Chomsky's biological influences
   d. Neural networks theories of language

12. Studies show that, when children start school with language deficits, the main cause is
   a. that these children predominantly come from specific socioeconomic groups.
   b. that these children lack supportive home, peer, and community environments.
   c. that these children predominantly come from particular cultural backgrounds.
   d. that these children mostly represent learners of English as a foreign language.

13. Ruby Gettinger, a Savannah, GA, woman who had a TV reality show, was known for her Rubyisms, like "I am humidified" (a combination of *humiliated* and *horrified*) or "hacky" (a combination of *happy* and *wacky*). How are these best classified linguistically?
   a. Idiolectal
   b. Dialectal
   c. Regional
   d. Familial

14. You are an SLP in a public elementary school. A group of African-American children are referred to you to evaluate for services to remediate delayed language development. They all use expressions like "She happy" and "There go Bobby." What are these evidence of?
    a. A common speech disorder
    b. A shared language disorder
    c. A regional dialect's usages
    d. A cultural dialect's usages

15. Regarding nonverbal communication in different cultures, which statement is accurate?
    a. Asian cultures tend to favor pointing at things or people using the forefinger, as Americans do.
    b. Middle Eastern cultures disapprove of using the right hand to transfer things or touch others.
    c. The forefinger gesture indicating "Come here" in America is very offensive in other cultures.
    d. Casual touching between opposite sexes is as appropriate in Muslim as in Christian cultures.

16. In speech perception, what is the smallest unit of sound in a language that we perceive?
    a. Formant
    b. Phoneme
    c. Frequency
    d. Vibration

17. In physiological phonetics, our audition (hearing) is processed in which lobe of the brain?
    a. Frontal
    b. Temporal
    c. Parietal
    d. Occipital

18. In acoustic phonetics, what is the greatest change from normal atmospheric air pressure?
    a. Period
    b. Frequency
    c. Amplitude
    d. Wavelength

19. In the anatomy and physiology of speech mechanisms, which structure is NOT a part of the upper air passageway?
    a. The oral cavity
    b. The pharynx
    c. The larynx
    d. The trachea

20. For a child to understand spoken language he or she hears, where must enough neural cell connections develop?
    a. Broca's area
    b. Wernicke's area
    c. Both of these areas
    d. Neither of these areas

21. An articulation disorder is a _____ disorder affecting the _____ level and involving _____ functions.
    a. Speech; phonetic; motor
    b. Language; phonemic; cognitive
    c. Language; phonetic; motor
    d. Speech; phonemic; cognitive

22. Children with Down syndrome often have some articulatory distortion, particularly with consonants like /s/. What is this due to primarily?
    a. Mental characteristics
    b. Physical characteristics
    c. Behavioral characteristics
    d. Unknown sources

23. What are individuals with hearing loss who speak *more* likely to have difficulty articulating?
    a. Vowel sounds
    b. Voiced sounds
    c. /r/, /s/ sounds
    d. All the sounds

24. Some individuals with cerebral palsy are more likely to have which condition(s) affecting speech?
    a. Dysarthria
    b. Speech apraxia
    c. Broca's aphasia
    d. A and B

25. Which is true about the speech of children who have fluctuating conductive hearing loss caused by chronic effusive otitis media?
    a. Their speech is unaffected because their hearing loss is not sensorineural.
    b. Their speech has normal intelligibility because the hearing loss fluctuates.
    c. Their speech typically is less intelligible, causing speech therapy referrals.
    d. Their being referred for help with speech intelligibility is very uncommon.

26. Susan is 7 years old. While her articulation was previously normal, this year, when asked her name and age, she says, "Thuthan" and "Theven." What is the MOST common and likely reason for this change?
    a. She has a developmental disorder.
    b. She has lost her upper front teeth.
    c. She has not reached the age norm.
    d. She has just suffered hearing loss.

27. Kenny has a phonological disorder. He pronounces his own name "Tenny." He pronounces "I gotta go" as "I dotta doe." These are examples of which place of articulation?
    a. He is substituting front phonemes for back phonemes.
    b. He is substituting back phonemes for front phonemes.
    c. He is substituting middle phonemes for front phonemes.
    d. He is substituting back phonemes for middle phonemes.

28. Cheryl is African-American. She and her parents regularly substitute /d/ for /ð/, for example, "I can do dis." What is this?
    a. A developmental disorder they share
    b. A phonological feature of their dialect
    c. A kind of phonological process disorder
    d. A kind of functional articulation disorder

29. Young children typically stop demonstrating phonological processes (i.e., typical, normal, predictable, developmental pronunciation errors) at certain ages. Which of the following processes normally ends at the *oldest* age?
    a. Saying "big" for "pig" or saying "pick" instead of "pig"
    b. Saying "efant" for "elephant" and "tevision" for "television"
    c. Saying "one" for "run" and saying "weg" or "yeg" for "leg"
    d. Saying "keen" instead of "clean" or "poon" for "spoon"

30. When a young child pronounces "cup" as "pup" and says "mine" as "mime," which phonological process does this represent?
    a. Devocalization
    b. Cluster reduction
    c. Consonant deletion
    d. Consonant harmony

31. If a child has a mild hearing loss between birth and 3 years of age, which of these is true?
    a. If the loss is mild, the child's language skills are not harmed.
    b. Language learning at this age does not need perfect hearing.
    c. This will interfere with a critical period of language learning.
    d. There is not enough research into mild hearing loss to know.

32. Which of the following behavioral or emotional disorders is MOST likely to coexist with a phonological disorder?
    a. School phobia
    b. Depression
    c. Anxiety
    d. ADHD

33. If a child consistently says "muh" every time he or she sees or is given milk, which of the following is true?
    a. This is an example of nonreduplicated babbling.
    b. This normally occurs around the age of 14 to 24 months.
    c. This is a typical feature of the later one-word stage.
    d. This is an example of vocalizations called protowords.

34. A typical development of children in the four-word stage of language development is more use of
    a. nouns and verbs.
    b. pronouns and articles.
    c. adjectives and prepositions.
    d. past and future tenses or concepts.

35. Which of the following is/are classified under motor speech disorders?
   a. Dysarthrias
   b. A and D
   c. Aphasia
   d. Apraxia

36. Tommy is 9 years old and has a vocabulary of about 1,000 words, can count up to seven things, and speaks in simple sentences. What is this description MOST typical of?
   a. Delayed development
   b. Normal development
   c. A language disorder
   d. Intellectual disability

37. Which of the following is more likely to cause a speech or language disorder rather than a delay?
   a. Hearing loss
   b. Muscular dystrophy
   c. Environmental deprivation
   d. Having been born prematurely

38. What kind of disorder does a patient diagnosed with Wernicke's aphasia predominantly have?
   a. Expressive
   b. Mixed
   c. Receptive
   d. Articulation

39. What kind of language do patients who are diagnosed with Broca's aphasia have more problems with?
   a. Receptive
   b. Academic
   c. Everyday
   d. Expressive

40. Which method of treatment for language disorders is found to be especially effective with children from socially disadvantaged backgrounds?
   a. Self-talk
   b. Modeling
   c. Cognitive
   d. Behavioral

41. For treating language disorders via strategy instruction, which of the following represents the right sequence for some of the training steps?
   a. Have the individual practice a strategy, then have him or her discuss and rehearse using it.
   b. Pretest the individual's strategy knowledge, then describe the strategy, then model its use.
   c. Ask the person to try the strategy in different settings, then have him or her practice using it.
   d. First model the strategy, then describe it, then have the person practice, then discuss this.

42. For whom is an IEP legally required to provide treatment for language disorders?
   a. Preschoolers and school-age children
   b. Infants, toddlers, and preschoolers
   c. Toddlers and preschoolers only
   d. School-age children only

43. Of the following principles for treating language disorders, which is MOST appropriate for infants, toddlers, and preschoolers?
   a. Promoting social interaction
   b. Increasing functional flexibility
   c. Slower treatment than in school
   d. The least restrictive environment

44. Of the following theories, concepts, and models of stuttering, which one is the MOST recent?
   a. Cerebral dominance theory
   b. Covert repair hypothesis
   c. Psychological theory
   d. Diagnostic theory

45. Which of the following is a characteristic of primary stuttering?
   a. Anxiety
   b. Blocking
   c. Awareness
   d. Rhythmicity

46. As an SLP conducting an assessment of speech fluency, which of these should you do first?
   a. Conduct an oral-peripheral examination
   b. Complete a fluency severity rating scale
   c. Conduct screenings of hearing and vision
   d. Collect family and developmental history

47. Which of the following is included among indirect therapeutic approaches to stuttering?
   a. Modeling a decreased rate of speaking
   b. Targeting pragmatics in everyday speech
   c. Practicing relaxed breathing techniques
   d. Not interrupting the stutterer's utterance

48. When comparing the therapeutic techniques of stuttering modification versus fluency shaping, what is true about stuttering modification?
   a. It gradually increases the length of the client's utterances.
   b. It can increase dysfluencies via more speech opportunities.
   c. It might incorporate the use of delayed auditory feedback.
   d. It begins with identifying stuttered words to modify these.

49. Which of the following is valid advice to parents for preventing fluency disorders in young children?
   a. Encourage the child to speak at a more rapid rate to promote fluency.
   b. Avoid unnecessary testing, which causes anxiety and a poor self-image.
   c. Avoid interrupting your child's speech, regardless how long he or she takes.
   d. Encourage the child to correct every single dysfluency that you notice.

50. Velopharyngeal dysfunction, which can affect speech resonance, can consist of velopharyngeal insufficiency or velopharyngeal incompetence (or velopharyngeal mislearning). Of the following defects, which can cause *either* velopharyngeal insufficiency *and/or* velopharyngeal incompetence?
   a. Enlargement of tonsils
   b. Neuromuscular disorder
   c. Irregularity of adenoids
   d. A history of cleft palate

51. Which is true about nasal air emission and its effects on speech and/or resonance?
   a. Its unobstructed form affects intra-oral breath pressure.
   b. Its obstructed form influences intra-oral breath pressure.
   c. Unobstructed and obstructed forms affect oral pressure.
   d. Both forms occur during the production of vowel sounds.

52. Speech featuring mixed nasality is characterized by:
   a. Hypernasality when producing oral vowels and hyponasality of nasal consonants.
   b. Hypernasality/nasal air emission on oral consonants and hyponasal nasal consonants.
   c. Hypernasality/nasal air emission on nasal vowels and hyponasal oral consonants.
   d. Hypernasality/nasal air emission on nasal consonants and hyponasal oral vowels.

53. Which of the following is true about what an intra-oral examination CANNOT assess?
   a. It cannot assess velar length or mobility in phonation.
   b. It cannot evaluate indices of oral-motor dysfunction.
   c. It cannot evaluate patient velopharyngeal function.
   d. It cannot assess the existence of an oronasal fistula.

54. Which statement is true about differentiating velopharyngeal insufficiency versus velopharyngeal incompetence?
   a. Velopharyngeal insufficiency is caused by physiological defects; velopharyngeal incompetence is caused by anatomical defects.
   b. While differences in symptoms exist, both velopharyngeal insufficiency and velopharyngeal incompetence are caused by anatomical defects.
   c. While differences in symptoms exist, both velopharyngeal insufficiency and velopharyngeal incompetence are caused by physiological defects.
   d. Velopharyngeal insufficiency is caused by anatomical defects; velopharyngeal incompetence is caused by physiological defects.

55. Which of the following surgical treatments for velopharyngeal dysfunction involves the injection of some type of filler?
   a. Retropharyngeal augmentation
   b. Pharyngeal flap procedure
   c. Sphincter pharyngoplasty
   d. None of these

56. Which of the following are MOST often caused by vocal abuse or misuse?
   a. Vocal cord polyps
   b. Vocal cord nodules
   c. Neither one of these
   d. Both of these equally

57. In addition to voice evaluation by an SLP and an otolaryngologist, which examination is MOST instrumental for diagnosing vocal cord paralysis?
    a. An intra-oral exam
    b. A perceptual exam
    c. An endoscopic exam
    d. None of these exams

58. Which of the following can prevent the MOST common cause for loss of speech due to removal of the larynx?
    a. Not screaming a lot
    b. Avoiding head injury
    c. Lower blood pressure
    d. Not smoking tobacco

59. You meet a post-CVA patient who says things to you such as, "My, don't you look pretty today," "What a nice dress," and "Do you think it will rain this afternoon?" However, she does not directly answer your questions. When you point at her watch, she says, "Looking at it, looking at it . . ." and engages in long, rambling discourses. What is she MOST likely to have?
    a. Wernicke's aphasia
    b. Broca's aphasia
    c. Global aphasia
    d. No aphasia

60. Which is accurate about people sustaining damage to the left hemispheres of their brains?
    a. The majority of left-handed people with this damage will have aphasia.
    b. Roughly half of right-handed people with this damage will have aphasia.
    c. The majority of right-handed people with this damage will have aphasia.
    d. Handedness regardless, most people with this damage will have aphasia.

61. What is the MOST frequent etiology of aphasia in adults?
    a. Dementia
    b. Stroke
    c. Illness
    d. TBI

62. Which of the following do Huntington disease, Parkinson disease, Wilson disease, and multiple sclerosis all have in common?
    a. All are progressive diseases wherein both motor control problems and dementia are possible or likely.
    b. All are degenerative diseases wherein both motor control problems and dementia always exist.
    C. All are progressive diseases wherein dementia exists and motor control problems are possible or likely.
    d. All are degenerative diseases wherein motor control problems exist and dementia is possible or likely.

63. For a patient with Amyotrophic Lateral Sclerosis (ALS), which speech characteristic represents the MOST severe level on the ALS Severity Scale?
    a. The patient vocalizes to express emotions.
    b. The patient speaks in one-word utterances.
    c. The patient can neither speak nor vocalize.
    d. The patient must undergo a tracheostomy.

64. A patient who has dysarthria secondary to ALS who can still speak intelligibly, albeit with repetition and effort, is a candidate for a palatal lift prosthetic device under certain conditions. Which of the following accurately represents one of these conditions?
    a. Velopharyngeal function and dentition are poor; symptoms progress slowly.
    b. Velopharyngeal function is adequate, but the patient manages saliva poorly.
    c. Velopharyngeal function is poor, but tongue and lip function are adequate.
    d. Velopharyngeal function is adequate, but tongue and lip function are poor.

65. What is the MOST distinctive underlying symptom of the flaccid type of dysarthria?
    a. Rigidity
    b. Weakness
    c. Hypertonia
    d. Incoordination

66. To where is the hyperkinetic type of dysarthria caused by neurological damage localized?
    a. The basal ganglia control circuit
    b. The cerebellar control circuit
    c. The lower motor neurons
    d. The upper motor neurons

67. Which of these is a motor speech disorder that causes difficulty in the brain's programming and planning of motor movements?
    a. Apraxia
    b. Ataxia
    c. Anoxia
    d. Hypoxia

68. Traumatic brain injuries (TBIs) can cause speech and language disorders as well as many other problems. Which of the following accurately represents recent statistics regarding TBIs?
    a. Approximately ¾ of the TBIs sustained every year consist of the most severe of injuries.
    b. The highest rates of TBI-related hospitalization and death are in adults aged 75+ years.
    c. TBIs contribute to only a very tiny proportion of all the injury-related deaths in the United States.
    d. In the United States, fewer than a million people are estimated to sustain TBIs annually.

69. Cognitive communication disorders are MOST typically associated with which of these?
    a. Damage to the left brain hemisphere
    b. Progressive neurological diseases
    c. Traumatic brain injuries (TBIs)
    d. Alzheimer-type dementias

70. ASHA finds that, for patients with traumatic brain injuries (TBIs), SLP services have been MOST effective in all BUT which area(s)?
    a. Attentional skills
    b. Memory retention skills
    c. Linguistic pragmatics skills
    d. Syntactic and semantic skills

71. In the swallowing process, which two cranial nerves each control the largest number of muscles involved?
    a. Trigeminal (V) and Facial (VII)
    b. Glossopharyngeal (IX) and Vagus (X)
    c. Vagus (X) and Hypoglossal (XII)
    d. Facial (VII) and Glossopharyngeal (IX)

72. In humans, head and neck anatomy undergo developmental changes from infancy that come to enable speech to develop. However, these changes also enable the danger in adults of aspirating liquids. Which of these anatomical changes is MOST related to enabling aspiration?
    a. The larynx moves to lower in the neck.
    b. The pharynx becomes vertically longer.
    c. The soft palate and epiglottis lose contact.
    d. The tongue and hard palate become less flat.

73. Which neuromuscular activities does the normal adult human processes of eating and swallowing involve?
    a. Both
    b. Neither
    c. Voluntary
    d. Involuntary

74. The original three-stage model normal eating and swallowing physiology was expanded to a four-stage model. Which of the following correctly represents the additional stage?
    a. The pharyngeal stage was divided into two stages.
    b. The oral stage was subdivided into two stages.
    c. The esophageal stage was divided into two stages.
    d. The additional fourth epigastric stage was added.

75. Which of the following causes of dysphagia is classified as a neurological disorder?
    a. Thyromegaly
    b. Polymyositis
    c. Poliomyelitis
    d. A neoplasm

76. Of the following, which can cause dysphagia secondary to affecting the connective tissues?
    a. Parkinson disease
    b. Cerebral infarction
    c. Myasthenia gravis
    d. Muscular dystrophy

77. Which of the following etiologies of dysphagia is obstructive in nature?
   a. Cleft palate
   b. Edentulism
   c. Xerostomia
   d. Esophagitis

78. Among serious complications of dysphagia, which of these is MOST related to aspiration of liquids?
   a. Dehydration
   b. Malnutrition
   c. Pneumonias
   d. Asphyxiation

79. If a general practice physician has a patient presenting with dysphagia symptoms, he or she may refer the patient to a specialist. Among the following specialists who work with dysphagia, which one is MOST likely to be involved (along with all or some of the others) if the dysphagia is secondary to GERD?
   a. Speech-language pathologist
   b. Gastroenterologist
   c. Otolaryngologist
   d. Neurologist

80. When a dysphagia patient is diagnosed with esophageal stenosis, which of the following treatments is MOST likely to alleviate the condition?
   a. Dilation
   b. Exercises
   c. Medication
   d. Diet changes

81. Of the following treatments for dysphagia, which one is LEAST common and MOST extreme?
   a. Surgery
   b. Endoscopy
   c. Feeding tube
   d. Muscle exercises

82. The process of hearing differs from the other sensory processes by being entirely _____ rather than _____.
   a. Chemical; mechanical
   b. Mechanical; chemical
   c. Involuntary; voluntary
   d. Voluntary; involuntary

83. What is/are the primary *sensory* part(s) of the hearing mechanism?
   a. Auricle/pinna
   b. Auditory meatus
   c. Tympanic membrane
   d. Cochlea and Organ of Corti

84. ASHA recommends that all children receive hearing screenings at what age?
    a. From 3 to 6 years
    b. 12 to 18 months
    c. 3 to 6 months
    d. Birth

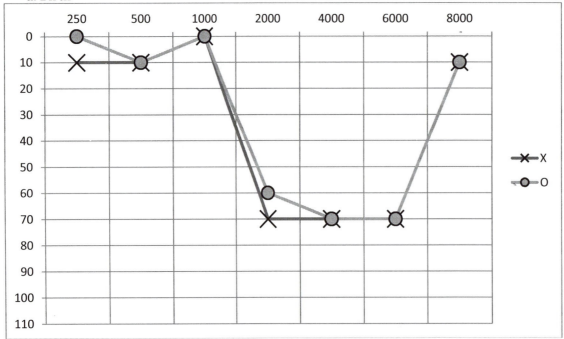

85. The audiogram above MOST represents which of the following?
    a. A left-ear conductive hearing loss
    b. Bilateral age-related hearing loss
    c. The hearing loss induced by noise
    d. A mild sensorineural hearing loss

86. What will a person with profound bilateral sensorineural hearing loss benefit MOST from?
    a. Bilateral hearing aids
    b. Cochlear implant(s)
    c. Both A and B.
    d. Neither A or B

87. The role of the SLP regarding hearing aids and/or cochlear implants for children with hearing losses and their families includes which of the following?
    a. Supporting them in attaining full-time device use as soon as possible
    b. Fitting the hearing aids on the child and testing their operation
    c. Monitoring the child's hearing loss and function of devices
    d. Performing the initial installation of cochlear implants

88. Which of the following conditions is MOST likely to make a child a good candidate for receiving a cochlear implant?
    a. The child has a mild to moderate hearing loss.
    b. The child has a profound bilateral hearing loss.
    c. The child has excellent hearing aid correction.
    d. The child's parents believe it will cure the loss.

89. Of the following, which statement is MOST accurate regarding counseling clients as part of the SLP's clinical practice?
    a. Most SLPs feel counseling is not their role even though their degree programs included counseling courses.
    b. Most SLPs did not receive counseling courses in their degree programs and feel counseling is not in their roles.
    c. Most SLPs feel counseling is within their role but received no counseling courses in their degree programs.
    d. Most SLPs have received counseling courses in their degree programs and feel counseling is within their roles.

90. Regarding student records and information that school-based SLPs might gather and use from other agencies, which law takes precedence in determining confidentiality requirements?
    a. The IDEA
    b. The FERPA
    c. The HIPAA
    d. None of these

91. When school SLPs have responded to research surveys, which do the majority of them see as the MOST frequent obstacle to communicating about students with other professionals?
    a. Student record confidentiality
    b. A lack of provider information
    c. The sizes of student caseloads
    d. Lack of time to communicate

92. Researchers conduct a meta-analysis of the findings of multiple studies investigating an intervention for stuttering. All studies included random group assignment of participants. With a 95% confidence interval, they find the intervention has an effect size of .854, with a lower limit of .507 and an upper limit of 1.202. Based on these data, which of the following is correct?
    a. Whether the effects were statistically significant is unknown with only these data.
    b. A causal relationship between the intervention and the effects can be confirmed.
    c. The average effect of this intervention was, at worst, none and, at best, moderate.
    d. The average effect of the intervention equals the effect for every individual study.

93. For individuals with intellectual disabilities receiving SLP services, which of the following is the MOST recent or current practice for determining when to discharge the client?
    a. When a plateau has been encountered in the effects of the treatment
    b. When client communication status matches his or her cognitive level
    c. When the client applies learned functional skills in everyday routines
    d. When the client feels that the effects of the treatment are complete

94. ASHA's criteria for discharging a client from SLP treatment include the client's motivation, tolerance for treatment, and things the client may do that interfere with therapy. How are these factors classified by ASHA?
    a. The client's behavioral status
    b. The client's goals and choices
    c. The likely treatment benefit
    d. The normative comparisons

95. According to reviews of the research literature, which of the following correctly represents a recent (post-2005) trend related to teacher referrals of students to school SLPs?
    a. Teachers have been over-referring students for voice and articulation treatment.
    b. Those reviewing the literature note the need for much more up-to-date research.
    c. Teachers are highly aware of clinical concerns with socially withdrawn behaviors.
    d. Those research studies of SLP services reviewed were all conducted in the 2000s.

96. State coordinators of early hearing detection and intervention (EHDI) report that too many infants who failed newborn hearing screenings still miss out on follow-up diagnoses and interventions. Regarding such follow-up, which of the following is true?
    a. There are plenty of well-trained EHDI staffs, but their communication with families is poor.
    b. There are plenty of EHDI facilities, but they lack enough personnel with sufficient training.
    c. There are plenty of good data management and tracking systems but insufficient facilities.
    d. There are insufficient data systems, facilities, well-trained personnel, and communication.

97. Which of the following is accurate regarding research findings about SLPs and writing professional reports?
    a. Most professors do not expect SLP graduate students to have scientific writing proficiency.
    b. Scientific writing instruction is equally effective if given earlier or later in the SLP curriculum.
    c. Studies have shown a need for profession-specific writing courses for SLP graduate students.
    d. Various studies have found that practice via assignments sufficiently improves writing skills.

98. Johnny's therapy goals include correctly articulating certain target phonemes 90% of the time. At the beginning of therapy, his correctness on these phonemes was 0% of the time. Over the past year, he has progressed to 75% of the time on all target phonemes. Which of the following would MOST clearly communicate this progress?
    a. An oral report stating enthusiastically how well he has been doing
    b. A written report stating that Johnny has made observable progress
    c. A line graph of monthly percentages along with oral and written reports
    d. A list indicating the percentage numbers for each month of the year

99. For children with dysphagia, which of the following evaluations uses technology the MOST?
    a. A pediatric feeding evaluation
    b. A clinical swallowing evaluation
    c. All of these evaluations equally
    d. A videofluoroscopic swallow study

100. According to the experience of SLP ASHA members and other experts, which of the following is accurate about using computer technology to reduce the time school SLPs spent on paperwork?
    a. SLPs can use computers for office work, but using them at IEP meetings is only a distraction.
    b. School systems frown on using e-mail to correspond with parents, teachers, administrators.
    c. You should avoid computerizing a master goal list because student needs are individualized.
    d. For students moving within state, uniform statewide forms reduce time learning their IEPs.

101. Of the following evaluation procedures defined under Part C of the IDEA, which reflects the need to establish the student's present speech-language status?
    a. The SLP administers an evaluation instrument to the student.
    b. The SLP interviews the parents and obtains the child's history.
    c. The SLP obtains student information from various informants.
    d. The SLP reviews the student's medical and education records.

102. When screening children for autism spectrum disorders (ASDs) specifically, which characteristic of the screening tool is MOST likely to be the LEAST realistic or diagnostic?
    a. Sensitivity
    b. Specificity
    c. Positive predictive value
    d. Negative predictive value

103. In which of the following areas does speech-language screening differ for children than for adults?
    a. In the principles that are followed for speech-language screening
    b. In the expected outcomes that may follow the results of screening
    c. In the individuals providing the speech-language screening service
    d. In the clinical indications for which individuals receive a screening

104. Which of the following is NOT a general advantage of standardized norm-referenced tests?
    a. Individualization
    b. Reimbursement
    c. Objectivity
    d. Efficiency

105. Which is generally true of diagnostic intervention and dynamic assessment in SLP?
    a. It is meant to determine effective treatment without therapeutic benefits.
    b. It is meant to build speech-language skills rather than to obtain a diagnosis.
    c. It is meant to build speech-language skills and determine effective therapy.
    d. It is meant to apply to all children with no benefit to special-needs children.

106. Of the following SLP activities for autistic children, which is MOST age-appropriate for an elementary school-aged child?
    a. Reinforcing the child's responding to hearing his or her name
    b. Practicing phrases and strategies for interacting with peers
    c. Teaching the child to ask social questions of his or her peers
    d. Practicing skills for successful responses in job interviews

107. Mendel first discovered by breeding pea plants that when the _____ for seed color is
_____, the _____ reflects the _____ allele.
a. Phenotype; homozygous; genotype; recessive
b. Genotype; heterozygous; phenotype; dominant
c. Phenotype; heterozygous; genotype; recessive
d. Genotype; homozygous; phenotype; dominant

108. Regarding cases of congenital deafness and hearing loss, which of these is correct?
a. More than half of these cases are caused by environmental factors.
b. The majority of cases of genetic deafness are not due to syndromes.
c. More cases of genetic deafness are secondary to genetic syndromes.
d. Syndromic and nonsyndromic deafness are always genetic in origin.

109. Abnormal phonetic patterns in early babbling and later speech are MOST associated with
which of these syndromes?
a. Cleft palate
b. Down syndrome
c. Fetal Alcohol Syndrome
d. Sjögren-Larsson syndrome

110. Of the following syndromes that can affect speech-language development, which one is
classified as a metabolic disorder?
a. Turner syndrome
b. Hunter syndrome
c. DiGeorge syndrome
d. Klinefelter syndrome

111. According to the ASHA Code of Ethics, which of the following can an SLP ethically do?
a. Use correspondence to deliver services to a homebound disabled client
b. Use correspondence carefully and thoroughly to deliver an SLP diagnosis
c. Use correspondence to give general educational information about SLP
d. Decline to provide professional services because of somebody's religion

112. SLPs can do which of the following without violating the ASHA Code of Ethics?
a. Share client records with another professional for consulting purposes
b. Give colleagues only professional, but not personal, client information
c. Give others access to their research activities before study publication
d. Provide service records to legal officials to protect the client's welfare

113. According to ASHA, which of these is ethical for the SLP supervisor to do if necessary?
a. Let a staff professional give services above his or her education level when he or she is
competent
b. Let a staff professional give services for which he or she is not trained but has much
experience
c. Let a staff professional conduct the research activities that he or she has the qualifications to
do
d. Let a staff professional conduct research activity he or she is inexperienced in but trained to
do

114. Which of the following is/are MOST important for selecting norm-referenced tests for evaluating language skills in preschool (ages 4 and 5 years) children?
    a. Use psychometric review to find tests meeting the majority of criteria
    b. Use both psychometric review plus data-based validation procedures
    c. Use data-based validation procedures instead of psychometric review
    d. Use psychometric review to find tests with high inter-rater reliability

115. As the SLP charged with conducting evaluations, you review information about an assessment procedure and read that it is considered highly valid but not highly reliable. What does this mean?
    a. It tests what it claims and intends to test, but it obtains variable results when repeated.
    b. It can be replicated and achieve similar results but tests another construct than it says.
    c. It is constructed according to valid principles but does not claim to test what it intends.
    d. It was validated but cannot be relied on to yield accurate results in any administration.

116. Which of the following is an example of a descriptive research design?
    a. A case study
    b. A cohort study
    c. A longitudinal study
    d. A cross-sectional study

117. Which of the following statements is correct regarding norm-referenced versus criterion-referenced tests?
    a. Norm-referenced tests measure more concrete cognitive skills and narrower performance ranges in homogeneous groups, while criterion-referenced tests measure more abstract cognitive skills and wider performance ranges in heterogeneous groups.
    b. Norm-referenced tests measure more abstract cognitive levels and wider performance ranges in heterogeneous groups, while criterion-referenced tests measure more concrete cognitive levels and narrower performance ranges in homogeneous groups.
    c. Norm-referenced tests measure more concrete cognitive levels and wider performance ranges in heterogeneous groups, while criterion-referenced tests measure more abstract cognitive levels and narrower performance ranges in homogeneous groups.
    d. Norm-referenced tests measure more abstract cognitive skills and narrower performance ranges in homogeneous groups, while criterion-referenced tests measure more concrete cognitive skills and wider performance ranges in heterogeneous groups.

118. Regarding the mandates of the IDEA and NCLB, which of these is true about increased accountability in designing assessments and treatments that comply with these laws?
    a. Students with disabilities have always been assigned the same curricula as the nondisabled.
    b. Academic performance standards for disabled students no longer mean grade-level content.
    c. These laws both mandate the inclusion of disabled students in state and district assessments.
    d. Using accommodations necessary to test and treat disabled students is not required by law.

119. Federal laws give all students the right to a free, appropriate public education (FAPE) in the least restrictive environment (LRE). Which of the following is true about the impacts of these regulations on delivery of school SLP services?

a. Comprehensive evaluation must precede addressing needs of students at risk for failure.

b. SLPs work with disabled students on special education goals but not on general education curriculum.

c. Achievement gaps for ELL, low-income, and culturally diverse students are not affected.

d. Special education services in schools now extend to disabled children below school ages.

120. During an SLP student's supervised Clinical Fellowship (CF), what is correct about Medicare's requirements for who signs the student's clinical reports?

a. In states licensing CFs, the supervising SLP must cosign these if he or she gave direct supervision.

b. In states not licensing CFs, the supervising SLP never has to sign or cosign such clinical reports.

c. In states licensing CFs, the supervising SLP must always sign reports as the qualified provider.

d. In states not licensing CFs, the supervising SLP only signs them if he or she gave direct supervision.

Answers and Explanations

1. C: Babies typically demonstrate imitation of the speech sounds they hear between the ages of 7 months and 1 year. Between birth and 3 months (A), they typically coo, goo, differentiate their crying according to different needs, and smile at parents. From around 4 to 6 months (B), they normally babble including speech sounds like /m/, /p/, and /b/; laugh and chuckle; gurgle; and vocally express unhappiness and excitement. From 1 year to 18 months (D), children normally begin uttering words, use one- and/or two-word questions and phrases, and acquire many different word-initial consonants.

2. A: Pragmatics is the domain of language focused on language use in social contexts, including how it affects others. Semantics (B) is the domain of language focused on the meanings of words. Phonology (C) is the domain of language focused on speech sounds and their relationships and systems. Syntax (D) is the domain of language focused on word order and sentence structure.

3. B: Typical motor skills development of a 1-year-old includes using the forefinger to point at and/or poke things and people. Cognitive skills (A) of a typically developing 1-year-old include searching for objects he or she has seen that have moved out of his or her sight. Sensory skills (C) of a typical 1-year-old include moving his or her body to music and imitating adult sounds. Language skills (D) of typical 1-year-olds include understanding simple spoken commands and uttering their first words.

4. D: English has primarily* an inflectional/fusional language structure; that is, it adds regular prefixes and suffixes to words to vary their meaning but also varies words for this purpose. Due to its many irregular forms, English and some other inflected languages are hard to learn. Languages with isolating/analytic (A) structures include Chinese, Indonesian, and Creole and Pidgin languages. These feature invariable words and strict syntactical rules. (*Note: While English is primarily inflectional, it has begun to evolve some analytic/isolating features.) Adults find analytic languages easier to learn than children do. Agglutinating/synthetic (B) languages include Turkish, Japanese, Finnish, Tamil and others. They are easy for children to learn. Their prefixes and suffixes are very regular. Amalgamating/polysynthetic (C) languages include Basque and many Native American tribal languages. They feature complex words, each imparting as much information as a sentence and are very hard to learn.

5. A: Phonology is the branch of linguistics concerning the patterns of speech sounds, their systems, and their rules in any given language. Phonetics (B) is the branch concerning the production, representation, and acoustic properties of speech sounds. Phonemics (C) is the branch concerning the study and development of the specific phonemes (= speech sounds) in any given language. Because only (A) is correct, (D) is not.

6. B: Theories of phonological acquisition termed *Universalist-Linguistic* maintain that children acquire phonological concepts as passive learners rather than actively (D). They also hold that phonological abilities do progress in a linear fashion (A); that all children universally develop phonological knowledge in the same way, without individual differences (C). The three incorrect choices all represent principles of cognitive theories of phonological acquisition.

7. C: The italicized phrase is an example of the future perfect tense of the verb. Tense is one grammatical category. Other grammatical categories include (but are not limited to) person (A),

that is, first person = I/we/us; second person = you; third person = he, she, it, them. Another is case (B), that is, nominative/subjective, where a noun is the subject, accusative/objective where a noun is the object, or possessive/genitive indicating possession, for example, "*John's* hat". And the last, here is number (D), for example, singular (e.g., "hat") or plural (e.g., "hats").

8. A: This is an example of classical conditioning. Ivan Pavlov pioneered it when he found that, by repeatedly pairing stimuli, for example, food that made dogs salivate, with a bell ringing, he could eventually condition the dogs to salivate upon hearing the bell alone because their automatic salivation over food had been coupled with the bell until they came to associate the bell with food. Operant conditioning (B) was pioneered by B. F. Skinner and involves voluntary rather than involuntary responses. For example, parents tend to reinforce (reward) their baby's babbling when it sounds like language, ignoring what does not sound like speech and thus eventually extinguishing it. Hence, they shape children's speech via successive approximations to language, a type of operant conditioning. Social learning theory (C) proposes that children observe adult speech and then imitate it, learning by social examples. Constructivism (D), which states that learners actively construct their own realities, is not a behavioral learning theory like the others.

9. D: Behaviorism (the theory) and behavior modification (the practice) are confined to observable, quantifiable behaviors. This is based on the premise that only an individual's external behaviors, that is, what he or she does, can be observed, measured, and therefore changed by others. Behaviorism and behavior modification do not deny the existence of internal states like thoughts (A), sensory perceptions (B), or emotions (C); they simply exclude these from being recorded or manipulated by others because others cannot observe them. Behaviorism maintains that, what we cannot observe, we cannot reliably measure and thus cannot consistently manipulate or change.

10. D: Piaget's theory posits four distinct stages of cognitive development, each with specific distinguishing characteristics and corresponding to approximate age ranges. Skinner's (A) theory of cognitive development is behavioral. It does not include stages but focuses on the premise that changes in behaviors over time represent learning and that this learning occurs through the antecedent and consequent events immediately before and after a behavior, which increase or decrease the probability of the individual's repeating the behavior. Vygotsky's (B) theory also has no stages and focuses on sociocultural influences as sources of learning. Bandura's (C) social learning theory has no stages either; it focuses on learning through observation, imitation of models, and vicarious learning.

11. C: Chomsky's theory proposes innate, "hard-wired" biological capacities like a Language Acquisition Device (LAD) and universal generative grammar enable children's language development. This supports the observation that children of all cultures develop language in the same stages and patterns around the same ages. Skinner's behaviorist theory, which emphasizes environmental influences (A), is less compatible: Children acquire language faster than they could through conditioning processes; they could not generate the infinite sentences possible via imitation; they learn without regular adult correction; and they overregularize irregular verbs without adult modeling. Whorf's linguistic relativity hypothesis (B) is also less compatible because Whorf proposed language differentially influences people's thinking by culture (e.g., Eskimo languages have far more words for snow than English). Neural networks (D) propose children learn similarly to computer systems with no preprogramming via exposure to many language examples. As this would vary among cultural contexts, it is also less compatible with universal language development than Chomsky's ideas.

12. B: Research finds that, when children begin school with language deficiencies, it is because their home and community settings and peer groups do not provide sufficient support or opportunities for language development. Language deficits are NOT found to prevail among certain socioeconomic groups (A), cultural backgrounds (C) or ESL/ELL children (D). Researchers point out that children from wealthy families can be deficient in language skills as well as those from poor families and that ESL/ELL children can excel in English at school just as native English-speaking children can perform below average scholastically. The prevalence of language deficits in ESL/ELL settings is more due to many of these children's English exposure being limited to school lessons.

13. A: Idiolectal is the linguistic term for language variations peculiar to an individual person. Dialectal (B) is the term for language variations peculiar to a certain geographic region and/or cultural group, for example, a South Georgia or East Texas dialect or the dialectal variations of urban hip-hop culture. Regional (C) also refers to the dialect of a specific region, for example, the Low Country dialect of South Carolina or the "Down East" dialect in Maine. The question never says Ruby got these expressions from her family, so they cannot be presumed to be familial (D); and in fact, nobody in her family taught Ruby these expressions, which she made up herself.

14. D: The expressions quoted are common to urban African-American dialects across the United States. They reflect conventions of this culture. Thus, they are not restricted to a particular region (C). They do not reflect a speech disorder (A), which would be characterized by misarticulation of speech sounds, aberrations in voice quality, or disturbances in rate and rhythm (stuttering). They do not reflect a language disorder (B), which would include problems with word finding or retrieval, constructing complete sentences, processing the spoken language one hears, and so on. (Note: Delayed language development can be attributed to processing disorders, intellectual impairments, and/or environmental deprivation, but it is separate from cultural dialect conventions.)

15. C: While it is common and accepted to use the "Come here" forefinger gesture in America, in other cultures, this gesture is only used to summon dogs and is found very offensive if used with humans. Asian cultures do not favor pointing with the forefinger as Americans do (B); they find this rude and instead point to things using the whole hand. Middle Eastern cultures do not disapprove of using the right hand to touch others or give them things (B); they prohibit using the left hand for these actions because they believe the left hand should only be used for personal hygiene purposes. Though it is acceptable in most Christian cultures, Muslim cultures generally find it inappropriate for opposite sexes to touch each other casually in public (D).

16. B: A phoneme, that is, a speech sound like a vowel or consonant that we represent with alphabet letters, is the smallest unit of sound in a language that we perceive. A formant (A) is a specific quality of a sound an individual produces, determined by the frequency region on the sound spectrum having the greatest relative intensity. A frequency (C) is how many times a sound vibrates the air, which determines our perception of its pitch, that is, how high or low it sounds. A vibration (D) is the movement of the air or other medium caused by sound production.

17. B: The temporal lobe of the brain is where audition (hearing) is processed and auditory perception occurs. The frontal (A) lobe is responsible for movement, including speech movements, and executive functions, like impulse control, language, judgment, reasoning, memory, personality, and so on. The parietal (C) lobe is responsible for integrating various sensory inputs into one unified perception or cognition and for coordinating spatial information. The occipital (D) lobe contains the primary visual cortex, processes vision and color recognition, and works with the posterior parietal and temporal lobes in achieving visual perception.

18. C: Amplitude is the maximum change from normal air pressure in the atmosphere created by a sound wave. We perceive relative acoustic amplitude as relative loudness. Period (A) is the time duration a sound wave takes to complete one cycle of vibration. Frequency (B) is how many cycles a sound wave completes per second. We perceive relative acoustic frequency as relative pitch. Wavelength (D) is the distance between the crests or peaks of a sound wave.

19. D: The trachea, also called the "windpipe," is below the larynx (C) and is not a part of the upper air passageway, which consists of the nasal cavities, the oral cavity (A), the pharynx (B), and the larynx. The trachea forks into dual bronchi that lead to the lungs.

20. B: Wernicke's area is a region in the human brain that must function properly for receptive language, that is, understanding the spoken language one hears. People who cannot understand what they hear others say (even though they are able to produce spoken language) owing to neurological damage in this area are diagnosed with Wernicke's aphasia. Broca's area (A) is a region of the human brain that must function properly for people to produce expressive language, that is, speaking and writing coherently. Because (B) is correct and (A) is incorrect, (C) and (D) are also incorrect.

21. A: Articulation disorders are *speech* disorders, affecting the *phonetic* level, which involves the *motor* functions needed for correctly producing vowel and consonant speech sounds. Language disorders that affect the *phonemic* level, which involves the *cognitive* functions needed for correctly organizing one's speech sounds into a system of phonemic or sound contrasts, are phonological disorders. (Note: Many people, including even SLPs, use these terms incorrectly or interchangeably.)

22. B: Children with Down syndrome have physical characteristics (to greater or lesser degrees) produced by the chromosomal abnormality that causes this genetic syndrome. One such characteristic is a thick, protruding tongue, which can often interfere with perfect articulation of consonants like /s/. Their unclear articulation is not caused by mental characteristics (A): Individuals with Down syndrome can have a wide range of intelligence levels. While there are also some behavioral characteristics associated with Down syndrome (e.g. stubbornness, affection), their articulation is not due to these. As physical stigma associated with Down syndrome and their effects on speech are well established, (D) is incorrect.

23. C: The consonants /r/ and /s/ are the most difficult to produce and have the latest age norms for children even with normal hearing to produce correctly. They present additional difficulty for hearing-impaired individuals because they are hard to lip-read/speech-read visually in production. Vowel sounds (A) are easier as they are all voiced (B) and their mouth positions are distinctive and easily visualized (/s/ is not voiced; /r/ is, but its mouth position is not as easily visualized and can be confused with other sounds). As some speech sounds are easier for those with hearing loss to learn and others are harder, (D) is incorrect.

24. D: Cerebral palsy is neurological damage to the brain's cerebrum, which controls the strength and coordination of the muscles used to produce speech. Dysarthria (A) involves muscular weakness and lack of muscular control of the speech mechanisms. Speech apraxia (B) involves deficits in programming and executing the motor movements of speech, despite normal muscular control and language comprehension. Broca's aphasia (C) does not involve loss of muscular or motor control but rather of the ability to produce expressive language: It involves damage to the brain's ability to retrieve verbal memory of words and their meanings, to organize words coherently, and to use words appropriately. It affects neural pathways for expressive language

functions; dysarthria and apraxia affect, respectively, speech muscular control and speech muscle programming and memory. Aphasias are more often due to strokes and other traumatic brain injuries than to cerebral palsy.

25. C: Children who suffer chronic middle-ear infections with effusion often experience conductive hearing loss due to fluid in the middle ear reducing hearing acuity. This hearing loss fluctuates according to how much or little fluid is present. Conductive hearing losses do not involve permanent nerve damage. However, hearing loss can impair speech, regardless whether it is conductive or sensorineural (A) and whether the loss is continuous or fluctuating (B). Approximately 30 percent of children referred to SLPs to help make their speech more intelligible are those with conductive hearing losses, so such referrals are not very uncommon (D).

26. B: It is most common for children to start losing their deciduous or baby teeth around the age of 7 years. The absence of the two upper middle teeth in front of the tongue interferes with producing /s/; without the dental barrier keeping the tongue in place below the alveolar ridge, the tongue is likely to advance to the interdental position that produces the /θ/ (devocalized "th") and /ð/ (vocalized "th") sounds instead, commonly known as a lisp. Sudden lisping around age 7 is not commonly caused by a developmental disorder (A) or new hearing loss (D) when the child previously had normal articulation. While the age norm for difficult consonants like /s/ (and /r/) is up to 8 years old, and Susan has not yet reached that age, a sudden change from normal articulation to lisping cannot be explained by this; if this were the reason, she would already have been lisping before.

27. A: The phonemes /k/ and /g/ are stops, produced using the same placement and positioning—with the back of the tongue against the velum in the back of the oral cavity—with the only difference being that the former is devocalized and the latter is vocalized. Because of the tongue placement, these phonemes are called *back* or *backed*. Kenny is substituting /t/ and /d/, which are the unvoiced and voiced versions of the stop produced by placing the tip of the tongue against the alveolar ridge in the front of the mouth, hence these are called *front* or *fronted*. He is substituting fronted phonemes for backed phonemes, not vice versa (B). Neither the /k/ and /g/ nor the substituted /t/ and /d/ represent middle {(C), (D)} phonemes, which are made with the tongue below (and touching) the hard palate in the middle of the oral cavity, for example, /ʃ/ ("sh"), /ʒ/ ("zh"), /tʃ/ ("ch"), or /dʒ/ ("j").

28. B: One feature of African-American Vernacular English, a dialect, is to substitute /d/ for /ð/ as described. Hence, this is NOT any kind of speech or language disorder at all but rather a phonological feature of this dialect. (Note: if there were a disorder, it would also not be developmental (A) because the parents also demonstrate it, unless the parents had been doing so since childhood.)

29. C: This is an example of changing liquid phonemes like /r/ and /l/ into glides like /w/ and /y/. The age norm for this phonological process to end in normally developing children is around 5 years. Voicing unvoiced initial consonants like "big" for "pig," or devocalizing voiced final consonants like "pick" for "pig" (A) are phonological processes that both normally end around the age of 3 years. The phonological process of deleting weakly stressed syllables like the "le" in "elephant" or "television" (B) normally ends around the age of 4 years. The phonological process of reducing consonant clusters by omitting one consonant (D) also normally stops around the age of 4 years.

30. D: The phonological process of consonant harmony occurs when one consonant in a word is influenced by another consonant in the word, so the final /p/ influences the initial /k/ (spelled "c") and the child changes it so both match. The /n/ in "mine" is influenced by the initial /m/. (Both examples are also made more likely by their similarity: In the former, /k/ and /p/ are both unvoiced stops; in the latter, both /m/ and /n/ are voiced nasals. In both, the difference is in place of articulation.) An example of devocalization (A) would be pronouncing "big" as "pick" (both initial and final consonants). An example of cluster reduction (B) would be pronouncing "straight" as "trait." An example of consonant deletion would be pronouncing "coat" as "co."

31. C: The period from birth to 3 years is a critical one for children to learn language. Infants and young children must be able to hear others' speech clearly in order to differentiate among various speech sounds. If they cannot, they will have difficulty mastering their own correct production of speech sounds. Even a mild hearing loss can interfere with discrimination of speech sounds, and hence with both clear speech and language development. Therefore, choices (A) and (B) are not true. Research into mild hearing loss demonstrates its correlation with speech and language deficits; hence, (D) is not true.

32. D: Research finds that ADHD (Attention Deficit Hyperactivity Disorder) often coexists with communication disorders. Researchers also find that many individuals with ADHD have neurological deficits in executive function, or higher-order cognitive skills. Phonological disorders represent deficits in processing patterns and systems in speech and language, which is a higher-order cognitive function. School phobia (A) is a social phobia involving abnormal fear of school. Depression (B) involves feelings of excessive sadness or hopelessness, social withdrawal, apathy, and so on. Anxiety (C) involves excessive worrying and fears. While any of these could and might coexist with a phonological disorder, none of them is found to coexist with phonological disorders any more often than other conditions, unlike ADHD, which is.

33. D: Protowords are early "words" used by young children which although they do not exactly match adult words, are still considered early words because the child consistently uses them to represent the same thing. Protowords differ from babbling, which may sound speechlike in its rhythms but does not contain words or protowords. Nonreduplicated babbling (A) means simply that the syllables vocalized are not repeated (e.g., "ba") versus reduplicated babbling, which does repeat syllables (e.g., "ba-ba-ba"). Protowords are features of the early one-word stage, which normally occurs around the ages of 12 to 19 months. The later one-word stage (C) features use of single, more-recognizable adult words like common nouns (e.g., *dog, hat, cup*), proper nouns (e.g., *Mom, Dad, Fido*), common verbs (e.g., *go, sit, come, hug*), and social words (e.g., *please, no, bye-bye*) and typically occurs around the ages of 14 to 24 months (B).

34. C: Children's language development focuses most on nouns and verbs (A) in the later one-word (c. 14–24 months) and two-word (c. 20–30 months) stages. In the three-word stage (c. 28–42 months), children begin to incorporate more adjectives (e.g., *funny, happy, sad, big, little*) and differentiated prepositions (e.g., *in, on, under, over*) into their language. It is not until the stage of complex utterances (c. 48–60 months) that they develop the concepts of past and future, reflected by their use of these verb tenses and other temporal terms like yesterday and tomorrow.

35. B: Dysarthrias and apraxia are both classified as motor speech disorders. Dysarthria affects muscular control of the speech mechanisms. Apraxia affects coordination of speech movements. Aphasia (C) is not a motor speech disorder but rather affects the cognitive processing of expressive or receptive language.

36. A: This description exemplifies delayed language development. Tommy is 9 years old and has the vocabulary (c. 1,000 words) of a normally developing 3- to 4-year-old. By 5 to 6 years, children normally have vocabularies of around 2,000 words, can count up to 10 things, and can speak in simple, compound, complex, and all other sentence types, while Tommy has not attained any of these by age 9. This does not represent normal development (B). However, delayed language development does not automatically indicate a language disorder (C), which can also include receptive difficulties with understanding others or expressive difficulties with communicating one's thoughts. Intellectual disability (D) is not the only cause for language delays. Additional causes include hearing loss, learning disabilities, premature birth, auditory processing disorders, apraxia, autism, and so on.

37. B: Muscular dystrophy, like cerebral palsy, traumatic brain injuries, and other neurological problems, can cause loss of muscular strength and control and produce speech disorders along with other symptoms. Hearing loss (A); environmental deprivation (C), for example, a child is deprived of hearing others speak; and premature birth (D) are all more likely to cause speech and language delays.

38. C: Wernicke's aphasia affects the receptive language ability to understand the language one hears others speaking. Wernicke's patients typically can speak fluently (though over time, the meaning of their speech tends to deteriorate due to lack of input and feedback) but cannot understand others' speech. Because patients have more trouble understanding than expressing themselves, Wernicke's aphasia is not an expressive (A) disorder, or a mixed (B), that is, expressive–receptive disorder. This language disorder does not involve an articulation (D) disorder, which affects speech pronunciation rather than language processing.

39. D: Broca's aphasia affects the expressive language ability to remember and retrieve words, construct sentences with understandable word order and grammar, and otherwise express what one thinks, feels, and needs. Broca's aphasia does not impair receptive (A) language ability, that is, understanding what one hears other people say. This disorder impairs all forms of expressive language rather than differentially affecting certain forms like academic (B) or everyday (C) language.

40. C: The cognitive approach to language remediation focuses on concepts and socialization rather than directly on language. It has been found to be especially effective with children who have been socially disadvantaged. Self-talk (A) can give more practice to children with learning disabilities; modeling (B) provides examples for children with limited awareness or understanding of their own errors to imitate; and behavioral (D) methods provide structure to children who have difficulty organizing their thoughts or need more systematic than targeted changes.

41. B: The SLP should first pretest the individual for prior knowledge about any strategy to aid in performing various language tasks. Then, the SLP should give the individual a description of the strategy, then model it for the learner, then have the learner discuss and rehearse the strategy, then have the learner practice using it, and then assign the learner to apply the strategy to different settings until the skill becomes generalized across situations.

42. A: The law requires that an IEP (Individualized Education Plan) be written, implemented, and updated regularly for preschoolers and school-age children. To treat language disorders in infants and toddlers {(B), (C)}, the law requires that an IFSP, or Individualized Family Service Plan, be written, implemented, and updated regularly. The IEP applies not only to school-age children (D) but to preschoolers as well.

43. A: Principles of language disorder treatment for the youngest children include early detection and intervention, greater parent involvement, and promoting social interaction through linguistic communication. For younger children, focusing on more functional results is more appropriate; increasing functional flexibility (B) is more appropriate for school-age children. Treatment of school-age children progresses at a slower rate than treatment of younger children, not vice versa (C). Treatment in the least-restrictive environment (D) is mandated by law for students in public schools, not for younger children, for whom the home or naturalistic environments are more appropriate.

44. B: The oldest of the choices is the cerebral dominance theory (A), an organic theory developed in the 1930s by Orton and Travis and proposing that stuttering resulted from lack of coordination between the brain's hemispheres when one side was not dominant. The diagnostic theory (D), a behavioral theory, was developed by Wendell Johnson in the 1940s and 1950s and proposed that stuttering was differentially conditioned by different parental responses to young children's normal dysfluencies. The psychological theory (C) that stuttering was a neurotic symptom best treated by psychotherapy has since been disproven by research findings that psychotherapy was not effective for stuttering; hence, it is not the most recent. The covert repair hypothesis is the most recent of the choices, proposing that stutterers have poor phonological encoding skills, leading to flawed phonetic plans, and that their dysfluencies are normal repair responses to these abnormal phonetic plans.

45. D: In primary stuttering, young children's speech may include many dysfluencies, but they occur rhythmically and easily without disturbing the flow of speech. Primary stuttering is characterized by the lack of awareness (C) of dysfluency typical of young children who have not yet developed metalinguistic awareness of their own speech. As they are not aware of their dysfluencies, they do not experience anxiety (A) over them. Anxiety over dysfluency causes tension, which contributes to the development of blocking (B), a feature of secondary stuttering.

46. C: The first thing you should do as the SLP assessing a child for speech fluency is to screen the child's hearing and vision. Hearing or vision deficits can have impacts on all speech and language problems, including stuttering. If such deficits are not diagnosed and addressed, speech therapy for dysfluencies will be ineffective. Obtaining family and developmental history (D) from the parents should come next. After gathering information from educators and care providers and reviewing school records for children in school and preschool, the next step is to conduct an oral–peripheral examination (A) to rule in or out any abnormalities that could contribute to dysfluency. Only then can you take measures of fluency, which will in turn inform your completion of a fluency severity rating scale (B).

47. B: Focusing on pragmatics, that is, how the stutterer uses speech and language in everyday interactions, is included among indirect treatment approaches. Modeling a slower speech rate (A), practicing relaxed breathing techniques (C), and allowing the stutterer to finish a statement without interrupting (D) are all methods of direct approaches to stuttering therapy.

48. B: The stuttering modification technique includes desensitizing the stutterer, decreasing the stutterer's anxiety, and decreasing the stutterer's secondary behaviors and speech avoidance behaviors. Because decreasing avoidance and anxiety produces more speech opportunities, with more opportunities, the stutterer is able to have more dysfluencies. This technique aims to enable "more fluent stuttering" rather than reduce or eliminate it. Changing the stutterer's emotional responses to dysfluencies enhances the self-image, which can facilitate self-monitoring. Gradually

increasing utterance length (A) or complexity, using DAF (C) in some programs, and identifying stuttered words and then modifying these (D) via shaping are all aspects of the fluency shaping technique.

49. C: According to ASHA, parents can help prevent a young child's normal dysfluencies from developing into stuttering by not interrupting the child when he or she is talking. ASHA also advises parents to give their young children plenty of time to speak rather than rushing them (A). Forcing more rapid speech rates does NOT promote fluency. ASHA recommends that, if parents are worried about their child's speech fluency, they should have the child tested by an SLP. Testing is less likely to cause anxiety or a poor self-image (B); increasing dysfluency is more likely to cause these over time. Parents should also not obsessively correct all of young children's dysfluencies (D), which may be normal. Normal dysfluencies often resolve without treatment.

50. D: A history of cleft palate can cause velopharyngeal insufficiency, which is caused by various anatomical defects including enlarged tonsils (A), irregular adenoids (C), cleft palate (D), and cranial base anomalies, like a deep pharynx or a short velum. It can also be a sequela of radiation treatment or surgery, for example, cervical spinal surgery via the mouth; nasopharyngeal tumor (radiation or surgical) treatment; adenoidectomy; or maxillary advancement surgery. Velopharyngeal incompetence is caused by various physiological defects, including pharyngeal hypotonia; velar paresis or paralysis secondary to cranial nerve or brain stem injury; neuromuscular disorders (B) such as myasthenia gravis; congenital or acquired neurological motor speech disorders like dysarthria and apraxia; and also impaired muscle function secondary to cleft palate.

51. A: The unobstructed (= no blockage) form of nasal air emission during speech affects the air pressure inside the oral cavity. The obstructed (= blockage) form has NO effect on intra-oral breath pressure {(B), (C)}. Air escaping through the nostrils occurs during the production of consonant sounds, not vowels (D) because it occurs during the production of sounds involving air pressure, which vowel sounds do not.

52. B: The feature of mixed nasality in speech is characterized by hypernasality or nasal air emission when producing oral consonants and hyponasality when producing nasal consonants. Consistent hypernasality or consistent hyponasality are especially noticeable in vowel sounds (and can also affect consonants), but mixed nasality is a characteristic of hypernasality and hyponasality, both specifically in consonant production: Oral consonants sound overly nasal, while nasal consonants sound insufficiently nasal.

53. C: An intra-oral examination can assess velar length and mobility during phonation (A). It can evaluate for any sign(s) of any oral-motor dysfunction (B), which the clinician should look for especially if the patient is diagnosed with any kind of syndrome. The intra-oral examination, however, cannot evaluate the patient's velopharyngeal function. This is typically done by first screening for signs of velopharyngeal insufficiency via inspecting for enlarged tonsils, a short velum, and so on; having the patient perform or attempt the Valsalva maneuver; and then conducting a combination of instrumental assessments (e.g., aerodynamic, videofluoroscopy, nasopharyngoscopy). The intra-oral exam can assess for the existence of an oronasal fistula (D).

54. D: Both velopharyngeal insufficiency and velopharyngeal incompetence cause inadequate functioning of the velopharyngeal closure, that is, of velopharyngeal dysfunction in general. However, velopharyngeal insufficiency is caused by anatomical defects, such as an overly short palate; a lack of tissue (as during repair of cleft palate); a submucous cleft; cranial base anomalies

causing a deep pharynx; sequelae of adenoidectomy, and so on. But, velopharyngeal incompetence is caused by physiological deficits, such as hypotonia of the pharynx; paresis or paralysis of the velum; poor overall muscle tone; or neurological conditions affecting speech movements, for example, dysarthria or apraxia, and so on.

55. A: Retropharyngeal augmentation is a procedure for repairing small, localized irregularities or gaps in the posterior pharyngeal wall, by injecting a filler substance such as collagen (e.g. Radiesse, Simetra, or Dermalogen), fat, and so on, into the tissue of the wall. The pharyngeal flap procedure (B) involves creating a flap from the posterior pharyngeal wall and stitching it into the velum to form a partial, medial closure of the nasopharynx. This operation is helpful for repairing deep, anterior-to-posterior (AP) gaps or medial gaps in the nasopharynx. It does not use filler injection. Sphincter pharyngoplasty (C) or sphincteroplasty is a procedure wherein the posterior faucial pillars and palatopharyngeus muscles are cut free and sewn together onto the posterior pharyngeal wall, creating a sphincter to narrow the velopharyngeal port. This is best for treating lateral gaps caused by "bowtie" closure of the port and treating narrow, coronal gaps. It does not use fillers. As (A) is correct, (D) is incorrect.

56. B: Vocal cord nodules are most often caused by vocal abuse or misuse, for example, habitually screaming; talking or singing for prolonged periods of time; excessive muscular tension; allergy symptoms; smoking; drinking caffeine or alcohol, which dry out the vocal cords and throat; or otherwise straining the vocal cords. Nodules are typically bilateral. Vocal cord polyps (A) are sometimes caused by vocal abuse or misuse but not as often as nodules. Polyps are also caused by gastroesophageal reflux disease (GERD) or acid reflux; hypothyroidism; long-term tobacco smoking; or one-time vocal cord trauma like screaming or yelling at a sports event or concert. Therefore, (C) and (D) are also incorrect.

57. C: An endoscope provides imaging of the vocal cords and their movement or lack thereof. An intra-oral exam (A) is limited to the oral cavity; the tonsils can be seen but not the vocal cords. A perceptual exam (B) typically involves assessing a speech sample from the patient. It can be used to detect symptoms of vocal cord paralysis (e.g., weak or breathy voice, becoming winded too easily from speech, etc., which can also be symptoms of other conditions); it cannot diagnose this condition definitively as it does not include imaging as endoscopy does. Because (C) is correct, (D) is incorrect.

58. D: Smoking tobacco (in cigarettes, cigars, and pipes), as well as chewing or "dipping" (holding between cheek and gum) tobacco, is a primary cause of laryngeal cancer (as well as cancers of the lips, mouth, tongue, salivary glands, esophagus, stomach, etc.). A common treatment for laryngeal cancer is laryngectomy. With removal of the larynx, the voice is lost. Avoiding screaming (A) can prevent most vocal cord nodules and some vocal cord polyps, which cause voice problems but not laryngectomy. Avoiding head injuries (B) can prevent vocal cord paralysis, which can occur secondary to head and neck trauma as well as to various diseases, tumors, certain surgeries, and strokes. Strokes are often secondary to high blood pressure, so lowering it (C) can prevent strokes, which can cause not only vocal cord paralysis but also aphasias, apraxias, and dysarthrias, which all affect speech and language. However, strokes do not lead to laryngectomies.

59. A: Wernicke's aphasia affects receptive language. The patient described still has fluent expressive speech, but she does not understand what others say. The lack of comprehension of input and feedback from others can make her spoken language somewhat irrelevant. She still understands gestural nonverbal communication. If she had Broca's aphasia (B), her expressive language would be damaged, and she would not speak so fluently, having trouble finding words and

arranging them grammatically into sentences. If she had global aphasia (C), she would have damage to both Wernicke's and Broca's areas of the brain and have difficulty with both receptive and expressive language. Despite her fluent speech and expressive language, she is not free of any aphasia (D) because she lacks receptive comprehension. Signs of this are her using "stock" social compliments and questions and not directly answering others' questions.

60. C: Left-hemisphere brain damage results in aphasia for the majority of right-handed people but for only about half of left-handed people. Therefore, (A) and (B) are both incorrect by reversing these proportions. Because areas in the left and right hemispheres control different areas of language processing, because handedness differentially indicates cerebral dominance, and because lateral innervation is cross-wired with the brain hemispheres, (D) is incorrect.

61. B: Strokes or cerebrovascular accidents (CVAs) are the most frequent causes of aphasia in adults. Alzheimer's, atherosclerotic, and other forms of dementia (A), various illnesses (C), traumatic brain injuries or TBIs (D), and progressive neurological disorders also can cause aphasia, but none of these does so as frequently as strokes do.

62. D: All of the diseases named are progressive or degenerative, that is, they cause degeneration or deterioration that progresses or advances over time. In all of these diseases, the patient always experiences problems with motor control, and in each, it is either possible or likely that the patient will also develop dementia.

63. D: The ALS Severity Scale progresses from normal speech—the lowest level of severity—to a few speech abnormalities; to more obvious changes and abnormalities in speech; to occasionally having to repeat statements to be understood; to often having to repeat; to some speech supported by nonvocal communication methods; to speaking only in single words (B); to no words but only vocalizations for expression (A); to the loss of both speech and voice (C); to ultimately being unable to breathe independently and requiring a tracheostomy to create an alternative airway for respiration.

64. C: The palatal lift is a prosthetic device that helps to lift up the palate in patients with poor velopharyngeal function. It is hence not indicated for those with adequate VP function {(B), (D)}. Patients' symptoms should be progressing relatively slowly (A) for them to be palatal lift candidates; however, this device is not indicated for patients with poor dentition (A) because their teeth must be adequate to support the prosthesis. The patient should also still be able to manage his or her salivary secretions adequately (B) to use this device. While the palatal lift is indicated to manage decreased VP function, the patient should still have adequate use of the tongue and lips rather than poor tongue and lip function (D).

65. B: The flaccid type of dysarthria is characterized by underlying weakness of the speech motor movements. Rigidity (A) or stiffness and problems with scaling movements are characteristic of the hypokinetic type of dysarthria. Hypertonia (C), that is, excessive muscle tone or tightness, is characteristic of the spastic type of dysarthria. Incoordination (D) of the speech motor movements is characteristic of the ataxic type of dysarthria. (Weakness, spasticity, and incoordination of speech motor movements are also characteristics of unilateral upper motor neuron dysarthria.)

66. A: The hyperkinetic type of dysarthria is caused by neurological damage localized to the basal ganglia control circuit. Neurological damage localized to the cerebellar control circuit (B) results in the ataxic type of dysarthria. Neurological damage localized to the lower motor neurons (C) results in the flaccid type of dysarthria. Neurological damage localized to the upper motor neurons (D)

- 33 -

results in the spastic type of dysarthria, and when this upper motor neuron localization is also restricted to one side of the brain, it causes the unilateral upper motor neuron type of dysarthria.

67. A: Apraxia of speech is a motor speech disorder caused by neurological damage localized to the brain's left hemisphere, where the motor movements for speech are controlled. Ataxia (B) is a lack of coordination; the ataxic type of dysarthria causes this symptom. Dysarthrias disrupt the brain's muscular control of speech movements, whereas apraxia disrupts the brain's motor programming of speech movements. Anoxia (C) means an absence of oxygen, which if more than momentary, causes brain damage. Hypoxia (D) means a lack of oxygen, which also causes brain damage when of sufficient severity or duration.

68. B: According to the Centers for Disease Control and Prevention (CDC), adults 75 years and older are the age group with the highest rates of hospitalizations and deaths related to TBIs. Approximately 75 percent (= ¾) of TBIs sustained annually in the United States are NOT the most severe injuries (A) but are mild TBIs such as concussions. TBIs contribute NOT to only a tiny proportion of all injury-related deaths in the United States (C) but to nearly a third (30.5 percent) of all such deaths—a significant proportion. In the United States, the number of citizens to sustain TBIs each year is estimated NOT to be fewer than a million (D) but more—approximately 1.4 million to 1.7 million (CDC, 2010, 2012).

69. C: Cognitive communication disorders are typical outcomes of many traumatic brain injuries (TBIs). This type of neurogenic language disorder is most often caused by a TBI. While damage to the brain's left hemisphere (A) could cause cognitive communication impairment, it is more often specifically associated with expressive language disorders like aphasia, or motor speech disorders. Progressive neurological diseases (B) could cause cognitive communication impairment but more often cause motor speech disorders like dysarthria and apraxia. Alzheimer-type dementias (D) can cause cognitive communication deficits, especially in verbal memory and working memory, but also notoriously cause global impairment beyond language and speech. Researchers published by ASHA attribute cognitive communication disorders particularly to TBIs.

70. D: TBI patients frequently develop cognitive communication disorders postinjury. These disorders typically involve deficits in attention (A); memory (B); and pragmatics (C), that is, the social uses of language. However, post-TBI cognitive communication disorders typically do NOT cause impairment of the skills for understanding and using correct linguistic structures—that is, syntactic skills—or for understanding and using language meanings correctly—that is, semantic skills (D). Thus, the reason that SLP services are not found effective in these areas is because these areas are typically not impaired with TBI-caused cognitive communication disorders and do not require remediation, so SLP services usually do not treat them.

71. C: The Vagus (X) nerve controls six muscles involved in the swallowing process: the levator veli palatine, palatopharyngeus, salpingopharyngeus, intrinsic laryngeal, cricopharyngeus, and pharyngeal constrictor muscles. The Hypoglossal (XII) nerve also controls six swallowing muscles: the intrinsic tongue muscles and the hyoglossus, geniohyoid, genioglossus, styloglossus, and thyrohyoid muscles. The Trigeminal (V) nerve controls four swallowing muscles: the masticatory, mylohyoid, tensor veli palatini muscles, and the anterior belly of the digastric muscles, while the Facial (VII) nerve controls three: the facial and stylohyoid muscles and the posterior belly of the digastric muscles {(A), (D)}. The Glossopharyngeal (IX) nerve controls one muscle: the stylopharyngeus {(B), (D)}.

72. B: The fact that the pharynx elongates vertically during normal human development from infant to adult means that, by adulthood, the foodway and airway cross in the pharynx. This makes adults susceptible to aspirating liquids, whereas in infants, the foodway and airway are separated except during swallowing. The growth of the oral cavity; the eruption of teeth; the descent of the larynx as the neck grows longer (A); the loss of contact between the soft palate and epiglottis (C); and the development of the tongue and hard palate from smaller and flatter to larger and more curved (D) are all developments that enable human children to develop speech.

73. A: The normal adult human eating and swallowing processes involve both voluntary and involuntary activities of the muscles and nerves. Therefore, (B), (C), and (D) are all incorrect.

74. B: The original three-stage model of normal eating and swallowing consisted of the oral, pharyngeal, and esophageal stages. The four-stage model consisted of dividing the oral stage into the oral preparatory stage, before the actual swallow, and the oral propulsive stage, wherein the tongue squeezes liquid against and along the palate and backward into the pharynx to begin the pharyngeal stage. The pharyngeal (A) and esophageal (C) stages were not divided into additional stages. There is no such thing as an epigastric stage (D).

75. C: Poliomyelitis (commonly known as polio) is a viral disease that affects the nerves and can cause paresis and paralysis. Hence, it is classified as a neurological disorder. Thyromegaly (A) is abnormal enlargement of the thyroid gland, which is classified as a structural lesion. Polymyositis (B) is classified as a disease of the connective tissue. A neoplasm (D) is any abnormal growth, whether benign or malignant. Neoplasms, like thyromegaly, are classified as structural lesions.

76. D: Muscular dystrophy is a disease of the connective tissue that can cause dysphagia by causing connective tissue and fat to grow into the muscles, causing hypertrophy (abnormal enlargement) and by causing muscle wasting and weakness. This can interfere with swallowing. Parkinson disease (A) is a nervous system disorder that breaks down the cells in the brain that produce the chemical neurotransmitter dopamine, which is necessary in the brain's regulation of movement. This cell breakdown reduces dopamine levels and interferes with movement-directing signals. Parkinson symptoms of muscular rigidity and slow movement can cause dysphagia. Cerebral infarction (B) is a type of stroke, which can cause dysphagia by damaging the brain areas involved in swallowing. Myasthenia gravis (C) is an autoimmune neuromuscular disorder that causes muscular weakness, which can result in dysphagia.

77. D: Esophagitis is inflammation of the esophagus. Inflammation can result from the irritation of GERD (gastroesophageal reflux disease), from a pill getting lodged in the esophagus or being difficult to swallow (pill esophagitis), allergic reactions, and so on. The inflammation causes swelling, which narrows or even blocks the esophagus, causing dysphagia. Cleft palate (A), a congenital structural abnormality, causes dysphagia by interfering with lip control in sucking; decreasing oral suction; and importantly, causing velopharyngeal insufficiency resulting in incomplete closure and thus nasal regurgitation. Edentulism (B), that is, the absence of teeth, prevents mastication (chewing); missing some but not all teeth makes chewing less efficient, leaving food boluses larger and harder to swallow. Xerostomia (C), that is, dry mouth or lack of saliva, interferes with the processing of food (saliva contains digestive juices), the formation of food boluses, and bolus transport during eating. Therefore (A), (B), and (C) are not obstructive in nature.

78. C: When liquids are aspirated, they go into the lungs instead of the stomach. This often results in lung infection, that is, aspiration pneumonia. Dehydration (A) is more related to the inability to swallow enough water and foods with high water content. If a dysphagia patient cannot swallow

- 35 -

enough for sufficient hydration, he or she is given supplemental fluids via feeding tube or injection. Malnutrition (B) is more related to not swallowing enough foods and liquids containing necessary nutrients, requiring supplementation. Asphyxiation (D) or suffocation is related more to aspiration of solids that block the airway, preventing breathing.

79. B: GERD stands for gastroesophageal reflux disease, a disorder of the digestive system. Gastroenterologists treat digestive system problems. The SLP (A) may also be involved simply because evaluating and treating dysphagia are included in the scope of SLP services; however, the SLP's involvement is not specifically because the dysphagia is secondary to GERD. An otolaryngologist (C) is a physician who treats ear and throat problems. Because the throat is included in the swallowing process, he or she may be involved if the dysphagia is high/oropharyngeal but not because the cause of the dysphagia is GERD. A neurologist (D) treats problems with the brain, nervous system, and spinal cord. The neurologist is only likely to be involved if the cause or effects of the dysphagia include these areas.

80. A: Dilation involves placing a device (sometimes an endoscope) into the esophagus, which carefully widens any narrow parts. Esophageal stenosis is a narrowing or partial closure of the esophagus. Dilation can alleviate this; it may need to be performed more than once. Exercises (B) for the swallowing muscles are used for cases of dysphagia caused by neurological, muscular, or neuromuscular factors—that is, disorders of the brain, nervous system, or muscles. Exercises can strengthen and retrain the muscles but would not dilate a narrowed esophagus. Medications (C) like antacids and acid reducers (proton pump inhibitors, H2 blockers) keep stomach acid from backing up into the esophagus in cases of GERD, heartburn, or esophagitis; antibiotics are prescribed for esophageal infections. Proton pump inhibitors may relieve symptoms caused by esophageal scarring or narrowing but would not widen the esophagus. Dietary changes (D), for example, eating or drinking softer foods or thickened liquids, make swallowing easier. This could help the patient work around the problem of esophageal stenosis but would not alleviate it.

81. C: A feeding tube is only inserted for dysphagia if the patient is unable to ingest enough liquid or solid nourishment for survival and health. This is seldom the case. Dysphagia secondary to esophageal obstruction often can be resolved via surgery (A) to remove the obstruction, or even endoscopy (B), a common and less-serious procedure without the recovery time of surgery, for example, if the obstruction is a foreign object or polyp. (A feeding tube might be a temporary measure when surgery cannot be performed soon enough or while the patient is recovering the ability to swallow.) Muscle exercises (D) are not invasive and often prescribed when the dysphagia is secondary to neurological, muscular, or neuromuscular conditions that cause muscular weakness or incoordination.

82. B: The process of hearing is entirely mechanical, while the processes of seeing, smelling, tasting, and touching all include chemical reactions rather than vice versa (B). Both voluntary and involuntary actions are involved in the complete hearing process (including the brain's auditory processing) rather than just one or the other {(C), (D)}.

83. C: The tympanic membrane, or eardrum, is the only part of the hearing mechanism that is actually sensory; that is, it collects sensory information from the sound waves that reach it. The auricle or pinna (A) intercepts sound waves and directs them through the external auditory meatus (B) or ear canal. The ossicles in the middle ear amplify the sound waves and transmit them to the eardrum. The cochlea and Organ of Corti (D) convert the acoustic energy of sound waves into electrical energy, which is transmitted by the auditory nerve to the brain for interpretation.

84. D: ASHA, as well as national and world health organizations, advocate universal newborn hearing screenings because hearing loss is the most prevalent congenital disability and often goes undetected without such screening and because early detection and intervention are crucial to prevent delays in language development and learning resulting from hearing loss. The ages in the other choices are not optimal because they are later than birth.

85. C: The audiogram pictured shows normal hearing at the low and highest frequencies, with a sharp drop in hearing acuity at the middle frequencies. This so-called "cookie bite" audiogram is typical of noise-induced hearing loss. The loss is bilateral, not left-ear (A) only. An audiogram for age-related hearing loss (B) or presbycusis typically shows a more gradual slope, with the least hearing loss at the lower frequencies, increasing to the greatest hearing loss at the highest frequencies. At the frequencies where there is hearing loss, it is NOT mild (D) but rather moderate to severe (60–70 dB).

86. B: Profound sensorineural hearing loss means that the hair cells in the Organ of Corti at the cochlea no longer function. This type of hearing loss cannot be remedied by hearing aids, which amplify the sound signal and require that the patient have sufficient residual hearing, which is not the case with profound hearing loss. Cochlear implants, however, are surgically implanted, bypass the outer and middle ears, and perform the function of converting the acoustic energy of sounds into electrical energy when the cochlear hair cells can no longer do this. Therefore, (C) and (D) are incorrect.

87. C: SLPs provide ongoing support to children and their families regarding hearing devices. This includes things such as helping parents with inserting hearing aids for young children, with attaining the child's full-time use of hearing devices as quickly as possible, with addressing the child's pulling out hearing aids, and so on. Fitting and testing hearing aids (B) are the roles of the audiologist, as are monitoring the child's hearing loss and hearing device performance. Initial installation of cochlear implants (D) is surgery and can only be performed by a surgeon.

88. B: Cochlear implants are generally recommended for children having profound bilateral hearing loss. Because it involves surgery, implantation is not advised for less-serious hearing loss (A), which can be treated with less-invasive methods like amplification, and so on. Cochlear implants are also not recommended if the child receives excellent benefit from hearing aids (C). Additionally, parental expectations must be realistic: Cochlear implants will improve hearing but will not "cure" hearing loss (D).

89. C: Researchers have found that the majority (e.g., 80 percent) of SLPs do feel their roles include counseling their clients, yet the same proportion of SLPs reported their degree programs not having offered any counseling courses. Research has not shown that most SLPs received counseling courses as part of their degree programs {(A), (D)} or that most SLPs feel it is not within their roles to give counseling {(A), (B)}.

90. A: ASHA reports that federal officials state that the IDEA (Individuals With Disabilities Education Act) takes precedence in determining the confidentiality requirements of student records. The FERPA (B) or Family Educational Rights and Privacy Act protects the privacy of student records maintained by agencies (or their agents) with federal funding but does not supersede the IDEA's confidentiality requirements. The HIPAA (C) or Health Insurance Portability and Accountability Act regulates the confidentiality of medical information via patient privacy rules but does not supersede the confidentiality requirements of the IDEA regarding student records.

91. D: The overwhelming majority of school SLPs typically report that the obstacle they find most often interferes with their communicating with other professionals about their students is a lack of time. The sizes of their caseloads (C) generally take a distant second place. Comparatively fewer cite confidentiality of student records (A) as a problem, and the smallest proportion are likely to attribute difficulty communicating with other professionals to a lack of provider information (B).

92. B: While correlation between two independent variables does not constitute causation, the data given here do confirm cause and effect between stuttering and the intervention investigated by all studies in the meta-analysis. This is because (1) in all studies within the meta-analysis, participants were assigned to groups randomly; and (2) the effect size observed by the meta-analysis was statistically significant* because the lower limit of the effect size was above 0.0 (0.0 = no effect). *Therefore, (A) is incorrect. According to the numbers given, the average effect of the intervention was moderate at worst, NOT none, and very effective at best, NOT moderate (C). The average effect found by the meta-analysis of all studies does NOT equal the effect for any individual study (D) or for all of the studies included.

93. C: In the past, the practice with intellectually disabled clients receiving SLP services was to recommend discharge when the effects of treatment hit a plateau (A) or when the clinician judged that the client had reached a communication level matching his or her level of cognitive development (B). In more recent years, however, experts have come to recommend discharging intellectually disabled clients when they have achieved the ability to transfer the functional communication skills they have learned in therapy to everyday life, as demonstrated by their performing these skills in the context of activities and routines of daily living (C). Both ASHA discharge guidelines and independent clinicians and researchers recommend, in addition to normative standardized test results and functional communication skills, considering the client's opinion (D); however, this applies to clients generally, whereas with the intellectually disabled specifically, some may be able to make and express this judgment with validity, but others may not.

94. A: ASHA classifies factors like client motivation, client tolerance of treatment, and any interfering behaviors of the client under the behavioral status of the client as one set of criteria for discharge. The client's goals and choices (B), also included under ASHA's discharge criteria, consist of factors such as the communication level the client desires and whether the client expresses a desire to participate in therapy or not. The ASHA discharge criterion of likely treatment benefit (C) includes factors such as whether the therapeutic goals have been attained, what kind of prognosis is expected for the client, whether alternative or augmentative communication methods are effective, whether the client's hydration and nutrition are functional, and so on. ASHA's discharge criteria additionally include factors such as comparisons of the client's communication status to that of normative groups (D) or to the client's pre-morbid communication when applicable.

95. B: According to literature reviews, such as one presented at the 2008 ASHA Convention, research into the topic of teacher referrals to school SLPs is sorely in need of more up-to-date studies. For example, researchers found that some of the studies they reviewed on this topic were conducted in the 1950s, 1960s, and 1970s, not all in the 2000s (D). Not only were these studies respectively over 60, 50, and 40 years old as of 2013; but moreover, speech-language services did not even figure prominently in public school settings during those decades. Another trend observed by those conducting recent literature reviews is that most teachers tend to under-refer students with deficits in areas like voice and articulation rather than over-refer them (A). Moreover, research reviewers find that teachers are often not even cognizant of the clinical implications and concerns of socially withdrawn behaviors and a variety of other student factors rather than being highly aware of them (C).

96. D: State EHDI coordinators have reported that the loss of follow-up diagnosis and treatment of many infants failing newborn hearing screenings is due to multiple gaps in the system, including insufficient facilities, not enough well-trained personnel, poor communication of poorly trained personnel with families, and not enough data tracking and management systems.

97. C: Research finds that graduate students in SLP preparation programs are not automatically proficient in the scientific writing skills they will need for writing professional reports, indicating a need for more profession-specific writing courses in SLP graduate curricula. Research finds that most professors actually DO expect these graduate students to be proficient in such writing skills without having been taught them (A). Research finds that, when SLP graduate students do receive such instruction, it occurs later in their curricula; yet, studies also show that such instruction received earlier in the curriculum benefits SLP students more by giving them more practice and skills refinement, so it is NOT equally effective whether given earlier or later (B). Research furthermore finds that practice via writing assignments alone does NOT improve students' scientific writing skills (D).

98. C: A line graph makes Johnny's progress from 0 to 75 percent clearly visible to parents, teachers, and others, likely including Johnny (unless he is very young or intellectually disabled). It most graphically and simply shows an obvious upward line. This illustration, together with a written progress report and an oral report summarizing progress, most clearly communicate progress as the results of SLP services. An enthusiastic oral report (A) is nice and may please parents but lacks any specific numerical measures as proof and quantification, as does a written report stating simply that he has made observable progress (B). Listing the percentage numbers for each month (D) is much harder to read and interpret, whereas the line graph makes the progress visually apparent even to nonprofessionals.

99. D: A videofluoroscopic swallow study uses barium and X-rays, whereby the SLP and radiologist collaboratively examine how foods and liquids move through the mouth, throat, and esophagus to the stomach when the patient swallows. In a pediatric feeding evaluation (A), the SLP reviews the child's medical history and feeding routines and the parents' concerns; observes the child's feeding and swallowing skills and mealtime behaviors; and tests various feeding techniques with the child. Technological instrumentation is not required. In a clinical swallowing evaluation (B), the SLP typically asks the parent questions about the child's swallowing problems; may ask the child to use facial, oral, and throat muscles while closely observing the movements; and may also observe how the swallowing muscles function while the child eats and drinks. Again, no technological instrumentation is needed. Therefore, (C) is incorrect.

100. D: When some families move within the same state, IEP forms can vary among school districts. Computer technology helps school SLPs use IEP forms that are the same across the state. This decreases the time needed to become familiar with different IEPs. Computers are a big help, not a distraction (A) at IEP meetings: SLPs can make changes to the initial IEP draft; use a projection screen for all attendees to see the text and changes they are making; and have a printer in the meeting room to print out the final draft for all to sign. Another way computers save time is on correspondence: Experts recommend using e-mail to correspond with parents, teachers, administrators (B), and others. Although each student's needs are individualized, it still helps SLPs to avoid "reinventing the wheel" by computerizing a master list of goals (C) for reference in writing IEPs. The technology makes it easier for SLPs to adjust or tailor IEPs as needed than to write goals from scratch for every plan.

101. A: Part C of the IDEA (Final Regulations, 2011) differentially defines evaluation and assessment. Under Evaluation, all four answer choices are included as required procedures. Answer choices (B), (C), and (D) are related to establishing the student's past speech-language status. Answer choice (A), administering a new evaluation instrument to the student, is related to establishing the student's present speech-language status.

102. C: *Positive predictive value* is defined as the proportion, out of all children screened and identified as at risk for an ASD, who actually fail the follow-up testing. The positive predictive value of a screening tool is inversely correlated with a disorder's base rate, that is, its prevalence. ASDs have comparatively low incidence, so the probability of a positive screening result's indicating the child actually has an ASD is lower. *Sensitivity* (A) is defined as the percentage of true positives, that is, of children identified as at risk by the screening who fail follow-up testing or are diagnosed with ASD. *Specificity* (B) is defined as the percentage of true negatives, that is, of children with negative screening results who also passed follow-up testing or had ASD ruled out as a diagnosis. *Negative predictive value* (D) is defined as the proportion of all children the screening identified as not at risk who also pass follow-up testing.

103. B: According to ASHA, both pediatric and adult speech-language screenings are conducted following the *Fundamental Components and Guiding Principles* (A). For both children and adults, the individuals providing the screening service(s) are SLPs with the requisite credentials and training, sometimes with the support of properly supervised SLP assistants (C). The clinical indications (D) for screening both children and adults are "as needed, requested, or mandated, or when other evidence suggests that they have risk for speech-language disorders associated with their body structure/function and/or activities/participation." However, pediatric screenings may result in recommendations for supports of normal development and prevention of speech-language problems; referral for comprehensive speech-language assessment, other assessments, or other services; or plans to monitor development, while adult screenings may result in recommendations for re-screening; comprehensive assessment of speech, language, or cognitive communication; or referrals for other tests or services.

104. A: Standardized, norm-referenced tests do not allow any individualization in their administration, which is a disadvantage, especially when testing special-needs or culturally diverse students. Advantages of using standardized tests, in addition to their enabling comparison to a norm group, include the fact that insurance providers are more willing to reimburse for known than unknown assessment instruments (B); that standardized tests are objective (C), whereas nonstandardized measures may not be; and that standardized tests are generally efficient (D) to administer, while less-objective, more-individualized tests often take more planning.

105. C: Diagnostic interventions, also sometimes called *dynamic assessments,* generally serve the dual purpose of building a child's speech-language skills while testing for which interventions are effective for that child via a Response-to-Intervention (RTI) model. So-called dynamic assessments offered by some clinicians also can benefit special-needs children (D) who cannot successfully perform on standardized test instruments. The dynamic assessment has the advantages of specialization and individualized observations not possible with standardized tests.

106. C: Age-appropriate activities for autistic elementary-school-aged children include practice with labeling feelings using stories and cartoons; teaching children to ask social questions of others; having children practice social communication together; modeling nonverbal communication; and using the child's special interests to prolong interactions. Reinforcing the child's response to hearing his or her name called (A) is more age-appropriate for young children with autism.

Practicing phrases and strategies for peer interactions (B) is more age-appropriate for preschoolers with autism. Practicing skills for successfully responding in job interviews (D) is more age-appropriate for high school students with autism.

107. B: When the genotype, that is, the genetic composition, for seed color is heterozygous, that is, inheriting two different alleles of the gene, one from each parent, the phenotype, that is, observable physical characteristics, reflects the dominant allele; that is, it masks the existence of the other allele. Recessive alleles can be passed to the next generation, but the trait (seed color in this case) is not apparent when the other allele is dominant.

108. B: More than half of the cases of congenital deafness in the United States are genetic rather than environmental (A) in origin. Of these cases of genetic deafness, the majority (70–80 percent) are nonsyndromic. Therefore, fewer cases of genetic deafness are secondary to genetic syndromes (C). While syndromic deafness is always genetic because it is caused by some specific genetic syndrome, nonsyndromic deafness is NOT always genetic in origin (D). It can be caused by genetic mutations or by environmental damage to structures in the hearing mechanism.

109. A: In children with cleft palates, research has found phonological deviations in their early babbling patterns, and phonetic deviations can continue in their speech as they grow older. Down syndrome (B) commonly causes an overly large, thick tongue, causing articulation difficulties and often causes delayed language development secondary to intellectual disability. Some Down syndrome children are found to show phonetic deviations as well as delays, but the former are not as notable as with cleft palate. Fetal Alcohol Syndrome (C) is associated with poor articulation, slurred speech, fluency deficits, absence of intonation, and voice dysfunctions, but not particularly with phonetic deviations. Children with Sjögren-Larsson syndrome (D) tend to have dysarthria and delayed speech-language development secondary to intellectual disability. They are more likely to be able to speak very little or not at all than to demonstrate abnormal phonetic patterns.

110. B: Hunter syndrome is a metabolic disorder wherein the enzyme iduronate sulfatase is lacking. This enzyme breaks down mucopolysaccharides (long chains of sugar molecules); without it, they build up and cause tissue damage. Among other symptoms, it causes progressive intellectual disability and progressive hearing loss, affecting speech and language. Turner syndrome (A), DiGeorge syndrome (C), and Klinefelter syndrome (D) are all chromosomal syndromes—not metabolic disorders—that can affect speech-language development.

111. C: Of the choices offered, this is the only one that an SLP can ethically do. It is permissible to give clients, family members, or prospective clients general informational or educational communications via e-mail, messaging, written letters, or other correspondence. However, it violates Principle of Ethics I of the ASHA Code of Ethics, Rule C, to discriminate in delivering professional services on the basis of religion (D), age, race, ethnicity, gender, gender identity, sexual orientation, national origin, or disability. It violates Rule K of this same principle to provide clinical services only by correspondence {(A), (B)}.

112. D: Principle of Ethics I, Rules M and N of the ASHA Code of Ethics prohibit allowing access to records of professional services they have given; research and scholarly activities they have engaged in (C); and products they have dispensed, except when authorized or required by law (Rule M) and revealing any personal OR professional information about clients served {(A), (B)} or participating in research and scholarly activities, unless it is necessary to protect the client's welfare (D) or the community, or it is required by law (Rule N).

113. C: The ASHA Code of Ethics, Principle of Ethics II, Rule B, states that SLPs in supervisory positions "shall not require or permit their professional staff to provide services or conduct research activities that exceed the staff member's competence, level of education, training, and experience." Competence without education (A), experience without training (B), or training without experience (D) all reflect conditions that violate this rule.

114. B: Research has long since established (e.g., studies dating back to 1992–1994) that psychometric review of tests for evaluating preschool language skills can identify such tests that meet half or even more of the psychometric criteria (A); and the review of the tests can attain high inter-rater reliability (D); and yet, these tests can still be inaccurate for differentiating children with normal language skills and those with impaired language skills. Researchers therefore advise evaluators of the need for using BOTH psychometric review AND data-based validation procedures, but NOT substituting data-based validation procedures alone for psychometric review (C).

115. A: *Validity* refers generally to whether an instrument tests what it claims or intends to test or not. *Reliability* refers generally to whether an instrument can obtain similar results over repeated administrations. Answer (B) gives the opposites of the correct definitions. Reliability (or validity either) does not mean an instrument claims to test something other than what it intends (C) or that it does not yield accurate results in any one administration (D).

116. A: A case study is an in-depth examination of a specific situation or individual and is a type of descriptive research design. A cohort study (B), a longitudinal study (C), and a cross-sectional study (D) are all examples of correlational research designs. A cohort study (B) examines a population sharing a certain trait over a period time. It is a sub-type of longitudinal study. A longitudinal study (C) observes stability or change in selected characteristics of given individuals over long time periods. A cross-sectional study (D) examines selected characteristics of a given population at one point in time.

117. B: Norm-referenced tests are better for measuring more abstract, higher cognitive levels; for testing heterogeneous (mixed) groups; and for testing a wide range of performance in groups with broad ranges of skills. Conversely, criterion-referenced tests are better for measuring more-concrete, lower cognitive levels; for testing homogeneous (uniform) groups; and for testing a more limited range of performance in groups with narrower ranges of abilities.

118. C: The IDEA (Individuals With Disabilities Education Improvement Act) and No Child Left Behind (NCLB) demand greater accountability of educators, including school therapists. Both laws mandate that students with disabilities be included in statewide and district-wide assessments. Before these federal laws increased demands for accountability, students with disabilities were NOT assigned the same curricula as nondisabled students (A). The 1997 and 2004 reauthorizations of the IDEA require disabled students to be included in the general education curriculum. Before these laws were enacted, school performance standards for disabled students were not congruent with standards for nondisabled students. However, with the accountability mandated by the laws, state school systems have had to change this to incorporating grade-level content into their academic performance standards for disabled students, not vice versa (B). Federal law DOES require using any accommodations necessary for the assessment and instruction and treatment of students with disabilities (D).

119. D: Federal legal mandates to ensure all students a FAPE in the LRE have expanded the populations served in schools and, accordingly, expanded the special education and related services provided in schools. School systems now provide services to preschool children aged 3 to 5 years

who have disabilities; and some schools also include infants and toddlers aged birth to 3 years. Another trend stimulated by the laws is to address the needs of students potentially at risk for failing academically before completing comprehensive evaluation to identify a disability (A) rather than after it, as has traditionally been done. Professionals, including SLPs, working with disabled students are specifically required by law to help them access the general education curriculum as well as with special education goals (B). Federal laws and findings of congressional committees are increasing pressure on schools to remediate achievement gaps for ELL, low-income, and culturally diverse students (C).

120. A: In states that license CFs, Medicare requires that the student's supervising SLP cosign the student's clinical reports only in cases when he or she directly supervised the student. Therefore, (C) is incorrect. However, in states that do not license CFs, Medicare considers the clinical fellow a student and requires he or she be supervised 100 percent by a licensed SLP, so the supervising SLP would be required as the qualified provider to sign everything the student writes. Therefore, (B) and (D) are incorrect.

Practice Test #2

Practice Questions

1. Receptively, at what age can children typically point to a few of their body parts on request?
   a. Four to six months
   b. 7 months to 1 year
   c. One year to 2 years
   d. From two to 3 years

2. Two- to three-year-old children normally develop the ability to understand and ask "Why" questions. Which domain of language is this an example of?
   a. Phonology
   b. Semantics
   c. Syntax
   d. Pragmatics

3. By the time he or she is a year old, a child typically responds to another's distress by crying or otherwise showing sympathetic distress. What is this development MOST closely associated with?
   a. Social skills
   b. Motor skills
   c. Cognitive skills
   d. Language skills

4. Within all world languages, which word order is used by the largest number of people?
   a. Subject-Object-Verb (SOV)
   b. Verb-Subject-Object (VSO)
   c. Verb-Object-Subject (VOS)
   d. Subject-Verb-Object (SVO)

5. What is/are the branch(es) of linguistics dealing mainly with the production, perception, properties, and description of speech sounds?
   a. Phonetics
   b. Phonology
   c. Phonemics
   d. All of these

6. According to the cognitive school of phonological acquisition theories, which is true?
   a. The phonological abilities of all children progress in a linear sequence.
   b. Children develop their phonological skills via active learning processes.
   c. All children acquire their phonological skills in the same way and order.
   d. In phonological acquisition, children do not show individual differences.

7. The words *mine, yours, his, hers, ours, theirs,* and *its* all represent which English pronoun case?
   a. Objective
   b. Subjective
   c. Possessive
   d. Ablative

8. A 3-year-old says, "I want 'pasghetti' for supper!" The parent says, "You mean spaghetti?" When the child repeats this correctly, he or she gets spaghetti. Eventually, the child learns to pronounce the word correctly. Regarding learning theories of language development, what is this an example of?
   a. Classical conditioning
   b. Social learning theory
   c. Generative grammar
   d. Operant conditioning

9. What are school-wide positive behavioral support programs MOST characterized by?
   a. Intensive behavioral intervention at the lowest tiers
   b. A stringent behavior modification system at all tiers
   c. A greater emphasis on prevention than intervention
   d. Giving positive reinforcement but never punishment

10. Of the following theorists of cognitive development, who stated that the requirements for learning are attention, retention, reproduction, and motivation?
   a. Piaget
   b. Bandura
   c. Skinner
   d. Vygotsky

11. Of the following, which statement is an argument against the behaviorist theory of language development as a result of conditioning?
   a. Children overregularize irregular verb tenses despite adults' correct examples.
   b. Children's rate of language acquisition is consistent with conditioning processes.
   c. Children can only generate a finite, fixed number of sentences in any language.
   d. Children acquire language through having adults constantly correct their syntax.

12. Which of the following is true about children who begin formal school with language deficits?
   a. Family preferences of news and current affairs over literature cause language deficiencies.
   b. Children's deficiencies in language development can compromise their social relationships.
   c. Assessment has revealed that most children with language deficits have lower intelligence.
   d. Children's language development is not influenced by peers' relative valuations of reading.

13. In an Amish family living in Pennsylvania, a mother tells her daughter, "Sally, eat your mouth empty before you say!" What is this version of the common American English expression "Don't talk with your mouth full" classified as linguistically?
   a. A familial variation
   b. An idiolectal variation
   c. A dialectal variation
   d. A regional variation

14. Tina's family came here from China. In school, Tina consistently drops the –s endings from plural nouns. What is this MOST due to?
    a. Tina's lack of familiarity with English as a new language
    b. The fact that Tina has an undiagnosed language disorder
    c. An idiolectal variation present only in Tina's English use
    d. Transfer from Tina's first language to her use of English

15. Which of the following statements is true about cultural differences in nonverbal communication?
    a. Native American and Middle Eastern cultures require eye contact in conversations.
    b. Vietnamese and Hmong cultures value admiration and compliments to their babies.
    c. Asian and Hispanic cultures find it rude or disrespectful to make direct eye contact.
    d. American and Asian cultures find it affectionate or friendly to pat a child on the head.

16. The study of speech perception has determined that the phonemes produced in human speech:
    a. are linear or sequential in their production.
    b. are invariant in waveform representations.
    c. are influenced and varied by co-articulation.
    d. are heard on a continuum as colors are seen.

17. Which of the following is true in physiological phonetics?
    a. The sounds we hear and produce are all processed within the same hemisphere of the brain.
    b. We process linguistic sounds in a different brain hemisphere than we process musical sounds.
    c. Our processing of spatial information is in the same brain hemisphere as our math processes.
    d. Analytical functions occur in the right hemisphere, while creative functions happen in the left.

18. In acoustic phonetics, sound waves are *always*:
    a. longitudinal.
    b. transverse.
    c. sinusoidal.
    d. complex.

19. In the anatomy and physiology of the hearing mechanisms, where are the ossicles located?
    a. Pinna
    b. Middle ear
    c. Ear canal
    d. Inner ear

20. In human children, which of the following brain structures involved in language is the *latest* to complete its development?
    a. Broca's area
    b. Wernicke's area
    c. The hippocampus
    d. The prefrontal cortex

21. A phonological disorder is a _____ disorder that affects the _____ level, entailing _____ functions that organize speech sounds into contrasting patterns.
    a. Language; phonemic; cognitive
    b. Speech; phonetic; cognitive
    c. Language; phonetic; motor
    d. Speech; phonemic; motor

22. What is unclear articulation often observed in some students with Down syndrome caused by primarily?
    a. Lower intelligence levels
    b. Physiological stigmata
    c. Behavioral problems
    d. Unknown etiology

23. Which of the following is MOST accurate about the articulation of individuals with hearing loss who speak?
    a. They must rely entirely on visual information.
    b. They produce devocalized sounds more easily.
    c. Vocalized speech sounds are easier to learn.
    d. Voiced and unvoiced sounds are equally hard.

24. Which of these conditions include(s) *consistent, overall* hypernasality of voice as a characteristic?
    a. Dysarthrias
    b. Cleft palate
    c. Speech apraxia
    d. (A) and (B)

25. Children with genetically based linguistic processing deficits that affect their speech are:
    a. among the majority of those referred to SLPs for help with their speech.
    b. among the minority of those referred to SLPs for help with their speech.
    c. among a smaller group than those having genetic speech motor deficits.
    d. among a smaller group than those with conductive hearing loss etiology.

26. Miles has recently come to America from his native England. He pronounces words like *thing, think, thank you,* and *other* as "fing," "fink," "fank you," and "uvver." What is the best explanation for this?
    a. An articulation disorder
    b. A phonological disorder
    c. A language disorder
    d. A regional dialect

27. When a child is said to have a *functional* or *idiopathic* articulation disorder, which of the following does this best mean?
    a. The disorder significantly impedes communication.
    b. The disorder is unique to this one particular child.
    c. The disorder's etiology has not been determined.
    d. The disorder is phonological in origin and nature.

28. Phonological process disorders are characterized by which of these?
    a. Errors in producing isolated speech sounds
    b. Patterns of errors in producing some sounds
    c. Omitting one consonant from initial clusters
    d. Both of the answer choices (B) and (C)

29. Of the following examples of phonological processes (= developmentally normal, predictable pronunciation errors typically made by young children still learning correct speech), which has the *youngest* age norm for its elimination?
    a. Pronouncing "fish" as "tish"
    b. Pronouncing "very" as "berry"
    c. Pronouncing "juice" as "deuce"
    d. Pronouncing "thing" as "ting"

30. At least half of a normally developing young child's speech should be intelligible to the child's parents by which age?
    a. 18 months
    b. 24 months
    c. 36 months
    d. 48 months

31. What percent of all speech problems are attributed to various degrees of hearing loss?
    a. More than 50 percent
    b. Fewer than 5 percent
    c. More than 10 percent
    d. Fewer than 8 percent

32. What is the clinical term for the condition commonly called "tongue-tied"?
    a. Glossolalia
    b. Microglossia
    c. Macroglossia
    d. Ankyloglossia

33. What is the typical age range when a child begins to combine two words, for example, "Where Daddy" or "Mommy shoe"?
    a. 12 to 19 months
    b. 14 to 24 months
    c. 20 to 30 months
    d. 28 to 42 months

34. In which stage of language development is a child who says "I can't tomorrow" and "It's behind you"?
    a. The three-word stage
    b. Complex utterances
    c. The four-word stage
    d. Cannot be discerned

35. Which of the following motor speech disorders is/are more localized in origin?
    a. Apraxia
    b. Dysarthrias
    c. Both are equal in localization
    d. Their localization is not known

36. Children between the ages of 1½ and 2½ years who are late to speak may have language delays or simply be "late bloomers." Which of the following have researchers found in following up with such children a year later?
    a. Children with normal receptive language were just late bloomers.
    b. Children using fewer gestures are more likely to catch up verbally.
    c. Children diagnosed at earlier ages have more negative prognoses.
    d. Children with language delays do not make progress every month.

37. What does an 18-month-old child who can follow simple directions but cannot say 25 different words have?
    a. An expressive language disorder
    b. Normal language development
    c. A receptive language disorder
    d. A language development delay

38. People diagnosed with Wernicke's aphasia have more difficulty with _____ language than _____ language.
    a. Expressive; receptive
    b. Speaking; understanding
    c. Receptive; expressive
    d. Producing; processing

39. What do people diagnosed with Broca's aphasia have more difficulty with?
    a. Comprehending questions others ask them
    b. Understanding statements made by others
    c. Discriminating among heard speech sounds
    d. Asking questions and/or making statements.

40. Recent research finds that speech-language therapy is:
    a. more effective for treating children's problems with receptive language.
    b. more effective for treating children's difficulties with expressive syntax.
    c. more effective with expressive phonological than vocabulary problems.
    d. more effective with expressive phonological and vocabulary difficulties.

41. Which statement is MOST accurate about the context of treatment for language disorders?
    a. Early interventions for young children not yet attending school should be in a clinical setting.
    b. For older children identified with disorders, by law, treatment should only be given in school.
    c. Treatment should be given in as many settings as possible including home, school, and clinic.
    d. In schools, integrating language goals in the classroom should progress to pull-out programs.

42. An IFSP is required by law for treating a language disorder in:
    a. a school-age child.
    b. an infant or a toddler.
    c. a toddler or preschooler.
    d. a preschool or school-age child.

43. For treating language disorders in school-age children as opposed to in younger children, which of the following principles is MOST appropriate?
    a. Promoting metalinguistic awareness
    b. Focusing on more functional outcomes
    c. Increasing the parents' involvement level
    d. Promoting language-based social interactions

44. Among the following fluency theories, which one attributes stuttering to the largest number of possible causes?
    a. The Demands and Capacities Model
    b. The Covert Repair Hypothesis
    c. The Psychological Theory
    d. The Diagnostic Theory

45. Which of the following MOST refutes an argument for neurological causes of stuttering?
    a. Research has found that more boys than girls exhibit dysfluencies.
    b. Children over 6 years old can demonstrate persistent dysfluencies.
    c. Stuttering is found to occur more commonly in twins than others.
    d. Stuttering has been found to occur more often in the left-handed.

46. Of the following measures made in a speech fluency assessment, which one is the MOST subjective?
    a. Stuttering frequency
    b. Stuttering duration
    c. Speech naturalness
    d. Rate of speech

47. Which of the following is included among direct methods of stuttering therapy?
    a. Changing a stutterer's environment
    b. Modifying parents' speech patterns
    c. Focusing on the stutterer's feelings
    d. Increasing pauses in conversations

48. When contrasting the stuttering therapy techniques of fluency shaping versus stuttering modification, which of the following is a characteristic of fluency shaping?
    a. Desensitizing the client from aversive feelings about stuttering
    b. Decreasing the stutterer's anxiety and avoidance behaviors
    c. Increasing the complexity of utterances via incremental steps
    d. Increasing the stutterer's self-confidence and sense of worth

49. Which of the following is true of ASHA's recommendations to parents for preventing stuttering in young children?
    a. Interrupting often will habituate young children to conversational give-and-take.
    b. If parents are concerned about their young child's fluency, SLP testing won't hurt.
    c. Limit the child's speech duration to prevent pauses, prolonging, repeating, "um"s.
    d. Correct occasional dysfluencies immediately and consistently, and they will cease.

50. Of the following resonance dysfunctions, which is characterized by a muffled quality, sometimes described as "potato in the mouth speech"?
    a. Cul-de-Sac resonance
    b. Hypernasal resonance
    c. Hyponasal resonance
    d. Absence of resonance

51. When air audibly escapes through the nose during speech, which of these applies/apply?
    a. The unobstructed form of nasal air emission has a high-frequency, high-intensity sound.
    b. The obstructed form of nasal air emission makes a high-frequency, high-intensity sound.
    c. Both unobstructed and obstructed nasal air emissions are high-frequency, low-intensity.
    d. The obstructed form of nasal air emission makes a high-frequency, low-intensity sound.

52. When mixed nasality is heard in someone's speech, what can cause this characteristic?
    a. Nasopharyngeal obstruction
    b. Velopharyngeal dysfunction
    c. Congenital/acquired apraxia
    d. All of them

53. Of the following instrumental assessments, which one is best for measuring the length and thickness of the velum?
    a. Aerodynamic testing
    b. Nasopharyngoscopy
    c. 3-D videofluoroscopy
    d. Nasometric analysis

54. Which of the following is correct regarding velopharyngeal mislearning?
    a. Velopharyngeal mislearning is a phenomenon unrelated to hearing loss.
    b. Velopharyngeal mislearning causes phoneme-specific nasal air emission.
    c. Velopharyngeal mislearning primarily causes hyponasality of the speech.
    d. Velopharyngeal mislearning is treated by speech therapy and/or surgery.

55. For someone with velopharyngeal incompetence due to dysarthria, which of these prosthetic devices would be indicated?
    a. A palatal lift
    b. A palatal obturator
    c. A speech bulb obturator
    d. None of these

56. Which of the following is true about common symptoms of vocal cord nodules or polyps?
    a. Patients with these voice disorders are unlikely to have hoarse-sounding voices.
    b. Patients often report symptoms of pains shooting from one ear to the other ear.
    c. Patients with vocal cord nodules or polyps rarely experience vocal or body fatigue.
    d. Patients have breathy, rough, harsh, or scratchy voices but no pitch range changes.

57. With enough training and practice, which form of alaryngeal speech is found to be clearest?
    a. Buccal speech
    b. Pharyngeal speech
    c. Esophageal speech
    d. None of these

58. Which of these is the clearest advantage of the electrolarynx over esophageal speech?
    a. The sound quality produced by the electrolarynx voice is more robotic.
    b. There are no alternative speech devices that are not held in one hand.
    c. The electrolarynx produces clearer sound than esophageal speech will.
    d. The electrolarynx has more immediate utility than esophageal speech.

59. You meet a post-CVA patient who appears to understand what you say but has difficulty responding intelligibly. Trying to describe a cat as Persian, she says "Skersian." She can speak in short social phrases, like "Hello, my darlings!" But, she frequently gropes for nouns, verbs, and adjectives she wants to describe things, and she rarely if ever utters a complete sentence, using mostly fragments that trail off into separate fragments. What does she MOST likely have?
    a. Broca's aphasia
    b. Wernicke's aphasia
    c. Global aphasia
    d. No aphasia

60. Patients with neurological damage to (the) _____ hemisphere are more likely to have other problems in addition to difficulties with their language and speech.
    a. Left
    b. Right
    c. Either
    d. Neither

61. In general, what do aphasia patients typically have more problems with?
    a. Speaking and understanding spoken language than reading and writing
    b. Speaking and writing than reading and understanding spoken language
    c. Reading and writing than speaking and understanding spoken language
    d. Reading and understanding spoken language than speaking and writing

62. Which of the following is correct regarding progressive motor neuron diseases?
    a. Progressive Bulbar Palsy (PBP) involves the degeneration of only the upper motor neurons.
    b. Spinal Muscular Atrophy (SMA) causes the deterioration of both the upper and the lower motor neurons.
    c. Primary Lateral Sclerosis (PLS) involves the deterioration of only the lower motor neurons.
    d. Amyotrophic Lateral Sclerosis (ALS) includes degeneration of both upper and lower motor neurons.

63. For patients having Amyotrophic Lateral Sclerosis (ALS), which of the following represents the MOST severe level of swallowing difficulty on the ALS Severity Scale?
    a. The patient aspirates secretions instead of swallowing them.
    b. Medications and/or suction are used to manage secretions.
    c. The patient requires tube feedings as supplements to eating.
    d. The patient requires tube feedings with nothing given orally.

64. When a patient who has dysarthria secondary to ALS still can speak intelligibly but often must repeat utterances to be understood, which of the following is NOT a recommended management technique?
    a. Having the patient maintain a slow rate of speech
    b. Having the patient engage in exercise regularly
    c. Having the patient exaggerate all articulations
    d. Having the patient use speech amplification

65. The neurological damage is localized to the cerebellar control circuit in which type of dysarthria?
    a. Flaccid
    b. Spastic
    c. Ataxic
    d. Hypokinetic

66. When a patient has apraxia of speech, where is the neurological damage causing it localized to?
    a. Basal ganglia control circuit
    b. Cerebellar control circuit
    c. Right hemisphere
    d. Left hemisphere

67. Apraxia of speech involves damage to which function of the brain?
    a. Motor speech coordination of movements
    b. Motor speech control of muscle movement
    c. Motor speech programming of movements
    d. Motor speech movements' muscle strength

68. Speech and language disorders and many other problems can be caused by traumatic brain injuries (TBIs). Statistically, which of the following age groups are MOST likely to sustain a TBI?
    a. Children aged 5 to 9 years, teens aged 13 to 16 years, and adults aged 75+ years
    b. Children aged 0 to 4 years, teens aged 15 to 19 years, and adults aged 65+ years
    c. Children aged 7 to 11 years, teens aged 13 to 18 years, and adults aged 50+ years
    d. Children aged 0 to 2 years, teens aged 16 to 19 years, and adults aged 80+ years

69. Of the following, which symptom(s) is/are LEAST associated with cognitive communication disorders?
    a. Impaired language content and form and impaired speech
    b. Impaired ability to participate in interactive conversations
    c. Impaired ability to interpret and express verbal pragmatics
    d. Impaired executive functions like planning or problem-solving

70. Which statement is true about strokes and other brain injuries involving the right hemisphere?
    a. Such injuries often cause right limb mobility damage.
    b. Such injuries often cause cases of visuo-spatial neglect.
    c. Such injuries often cause deficits of the right visual field.
    d. Such injuries often cause no figurative language problems.

71. Which of the cranial nerves controls the smallest number of muscles involved in the adult human swallowing process?
    a. The Hypoglossal (XII) nerve
    b. The Trigeminal (V) nerve
    c. The Glossopharyngeal (IX) nerve
    d. The Facial (VII) nerve

72. In human anatomical structures related to swallowing, which of the following closes the upper esophageal sphincter (UES)?
    a. The pharynx constrictor muscles
    b. The submental muscles
    c. The pyriform recesses
    d. The cricopharyngeus muscle

73. How many muscles and nerves does the normal adult human process of eating and swallowing involve?
    a. More than 40
    b. Fewer than 20
    c. More than 30
    d. Fewer than 10

74. Why was the process model of the physiology of normal adult human eating and swallowing adopted to replace the previous four-stage sequential model?
    a. The four-stage model did not include enough stages to cover the whole process.
    b. The four-stage model covered swallowing of liquids but not swallowing of solids.
    c. The four-stage model described a process that later imaging proved inaccurate.
    d. The four-stage model described overlapping stages rather than discrete stages.

75. A patient has developed dysphagia, and the cause is found to be iatrogenic. Which of the following etiologies would LEAST fit this diagnosis?
    a. Caustic materials
    b. Surgical resection
    c. Radiation fibrosis
    d. Drug side effects

76. Which condition narrows and hardens esophageal tissues and can weaken the lower esophageal muscle, which can cause dysphagia?
    a. Multiple sclerosis
    b. Esophageal spasm
    c. Dermatomyositis
    d. Scleroderma

77. Which of the following causes dysphagia for functional rather than obstructive reasons?
    a. Diverticulitis
    b. Chemoradiation
    c. Cervical osteophytes
    d. Gastroesophageal Reflux Disease (GERD)

78. Of the following impairments in airway protection related to swallowing, which is MOST likely to cause aspiration *during* swallowing rather than before or after swallowing?
    a. Liquids entering the pharynx too soon due to poor oral containment
    b. Delayed laryngeal closure after a bolus is propelled into the pharynx
    c. Poor vocal fold closure from paralysis, weakness, or anatomical fixation
    d. Residual material accumulated in the pharynx and not all swallowed

79. A patient is diagnosed with dysphagia, but testing is required to determine its cause. Of the following tests, which one measures the patient's esophageal pressure during swallowing?
    a. Manometry
    b. Laryngoscopy
    c. pH monitoring
    d. Esophagoscopy

80. If a dysphagia patient is found to have some esophageal obstruction, which of the following treatment options would be indicated?
    a. Dilation and/or medication
    b. Endoscopy and/or surgery
    c. Exercises and/or medication
    d. Diet change and/or exercises

81. A patient is diagnosed with inoperable esophageal cancer, and radiation and chemotherapy are insufficient without surgery. Which other treatment is preferable?
    a. Botulinum toxin
    b. Endoscopic dilation
    c. The insertion of a stent
    d. A proton pump inhibitor

82. The process of hearing involves _____ reactions, while the other sensory processes involve _____ reactions.
    a. Voluntary; involuntary
    b. Involuntary; voluntary
    c. Chemical; mechanical
    d. Mechanical; chemical

83. What does the stapedius reflex do?
    a. Amplifies sound waves for hearing
    b. Activates the stapes so it vibrates
    c. Protects the ears from loud noises
    d. Enables us to hear our own voices

84. Hearing screening is recommended for which newborn infants?
    a. Babies at risk of hearing loss
    b. Every single baby who is born
    c. Only babies in neonatal ICUs
    d. None as it is too early to screen

85. An individual's audiogram shows a level of 10 dB in the left ear at 500 Hz; 60 dB in the right ear at 500 Hz; 50 dB in the left ear at 8000 Hz; and 90 dB in the right ear at 8000 Hz. How would this person's hearing loss be described?
    a. Asymmetrical
    b. Unilateral
    c. Symmetrical
    d. High-frequency

86. Hearing aids _____ sounds, whereas cochlear implants _____ sounds.
    a. Convert; amplify
    b. Amplify; convert
    c. Transmit; sharpen
    d. Sharpen; transmit

87. When parents have a baby with profound hearing loss and are trying to decide whether to use ASL (American Sign Language) or hearing aids until the baby is of the age recommended for cochlear implants, which of these is most accurate about the role of the SLP?
    a. Counseling parents about ASL should only be by a deaf educator.
    b. Only the surgeon to do cochlear implantation should advise them.
    c. It is within the scope of the SLP to counsel parents on this decision.
    d. Only the audiologist should counsel the parents about hearing aids.

88. Which of the following adults would be the best candidate for cochlear implants?
    a. One who hears very well using hearing aids
    b. One with moderate unilateral hearing loss
    c. One who strongly embraces deaf culture
    d. One who lost his or her hearing in adolescence

89. Which statement is most accurate regarding the role of counseling in an SLP's work?
    a. For SLPs, providing counseling consists of giving information, instruction, and advice.
    b. SLP clinicians can increase the effectiveness of their other treatments via counseling.
    c. SLPs who provide counseling take the place of psychologists or professional counselors.
    d. Counseling by SLPs does not address the emotional impact of the client's impairment.

90. The confidentiality provisions of the IDEA include that every participating agency keep records of parties obtaining access to a child's education records including name, date, and purpose for which the party is authorized to use the records. What types of access does this include?
    a. Access by the parents of the child of the records used
    b. Access by any employees of the participating agency
    c. Access by both the parents and agency employees
    d. Access by neither parents nor agency employees

91. School SLPs have reported to research surveys that, in receiving information about students' therapy goals, progress in therapy, and behavior management, the two MOST common methods of their getting this information from professionals at other facilities are:
    a. telephone calls and parental reports.
    b. reports from the parents and e-mails.
    c. formal reports and parental reports.
    d. telephone calls and formal reports.

92. When interpreting data from a meta-analysis of multiple studies investigating interventions for stuttering, which of the following statements is MOST accurate?
    a. If one study finds an intervention has small or statistically nonsignificant effects, that intervention should be discarded.
    b. If one study finds an intervention has large or statistically significant effects, that intervention should be adopted.
    c. With differing research methodology and confounding variables, one study sometimes suffices, or several are needed.
    d. Just as diagnoses require multiple assessments, adopting an intervention requires the findings of multiple investigations.

93. In which of the following practice settings is the SLP the one responsible for deciding when to terminate speech-language therapy?
    a. In Birth-to-3 programs
    b. In public school systems
    c. In health care systems
    d. In none of these

94. Which of the following is true about ASHA's criteria for discharging SLP clients?
    a. These criteria are client centered rather than disability centered.
    b. These criteria reflect functional measures, not standardized tests.
    c. These criteria include whether treatment resources are available.
    d. These criteria do not address the disorder's impact on daily living.

95. According to research, which of the following is most accurate relative to referrals by public school teachers of students to school SLPs for potential speech or language disorders?
    a. SLP evaluations are more important than teacher referrals as teachers are not SLP experts.
    b. It is important for the relationship between school SLPs and teachers to be made stronger.
    c. Because of their training, SLPs are more likely to be first to notice some student behaviors.
    d. Numerous research studies find teachers tend to over-refer students to SLPs for evaluation.

96. According to state EHDI (early hearing detection and intervention) coordinators, various gaps in the system cause many newborns failing hearing screenings to be lost to follow-up diagnosis and treatment. Which of the following is true about some of these gaps?
    a. Inadequate insurance reimbursements for diagnosis often interfere with infant services.
    b. Privacy regulations protect families and are not found to present obstacles to follow-up.
    c. Many families are located far from EHDI facilities but still manage to pursue follow-up.
    d. Follow-up for at-risk babies is lacking, but EHDI programs screen far more preschoolers.

97. According to ASHA's treatment efficacy summaries, which of the following populations demonstrated the largest proportion of gain from SLP interventions?
    a. Patients who had aphasia secondary to left-hemisphere strokes
    b. Preschool children with diagnoses of autism spectrum disorders
    c. Preschool-aged children identified as having language disorders
    d. Dysphagic adults starting treatment at home with feeding tubes

98. As an SLP, you implement the first stuttering therapy program for a client. After collecting data for three months, you find that measures of the client's stuttering levels, while inconsistent, always reflect less than 20 percent improvement. What does this mean?
    a. These results show no more improvement than could have occurred by chance.
    b. These results show that the client is making adequate albeit slow improvement.
    c. These results show your measurements are inaccurate and need to be changed.
    d. These results show your therapy is ineffective and must be discarded or replaced.

99. For testing neurological disorders affecting speech and language, which instrumental technology can *noninvasively* show the relative *metabolic* activity levels of various parts of the brain?
    a. fMRI
    b. MRI
    c. EEG
    d. PET

100. Computer technology is now incorporated into therapy for SLPs and clients and students, including which of these?
    a. Independent client and student practice
    b. Research into professional practices
    c. Promoting client and family self-advocacy
    d. All these uses and more

101. In formulating recommendations for treatment and service delivery, which of the following would the SLP do first?
    a. Decide which treatment materials are most appropriate and effective with the rationale
    b. Decide which theoretical service delivery model is most appropriate for the client's needs
    c. Decide which design and data collection methods can best measure treatment efficacy
    d. Decide which treatment methods are most appropriate and effective and give a rationale

102. Which of the following is true regarding techniques for SLPs to interview clients and family members of clients?
    a. Questions are a primary interviewing behavior for increasing responses.
    b. Closed questions are better because they direct more specific responses.
    c. Open questions let the client or family member respond in various ways.
    d. Silence is a secondary interviewing behavior by its decreasing responses.

103. Which of the following is an advantage of authentic assessments like language sampling, simulations, video recording, and so on, as compared to standardized assessments?
    a. This approach usually does not enable the assessor to know its reliability and validity.
    b. This approach demands very high levels of clinical experience and skill to implement.
    c. This approach involves more time for planning and may be less objective or practical.
    d. This approach is flexible and can be individualized for special-needs or diverse clients.

104. Which of the following is true about norm-referenced, standardized test instruments?
    a. These tests are better for showing what someone knows than how he or she learns.
    b. These tests require much clinical experience and skill to administer and score.
    c. These tests retain their validity and reliability regardless of how administered.
    d. These tests are equally applicable with linguistically or culturally diverse students.

105. Which is true about *dynamic assessments* or diagnostic interventions in SLP?
    a. These can help test children with ASDs, ID, and other developmental disabilities.
    b. These are very similar to standardized, norm-referenced assessment instruments.
    c. These are unlikely to use observations of the child's spontaneous communication.
    d. These are likely to take less time to administer than standardized test instruments.

106. Of the following SLP activities for children on the autism spectrum, which is most age-appropriate for a high school student?
    a. Working on identifying emotions using favorite books, characters, or drawings
    b. Working on strategies to respond to unpredictable individuals and interactions
    c. Working on turn taking in games like Memory to prepare for conversations
    d. Working on saying or signing *more* to encourage functional communication

107. Of the following statements, which one reflects the genetic principle of independent assortment?
    a. One allele from each parent's pair of alleles for a trait passes to the offspring.
    b. The process of meiosis that forms sex cells affects the inheritance of alleles.
    c. The genes for certain inherited traits are located on different chromosomes.
    d. Inheriting a particular trait does not influence inheritance of a different trait.

108. Among the following inheritance patterns of nonsyndromic deafness, which is most common?
    a. Mitochondrial change
    b. Autosomal dominant
    c. The X-linked pattern
    d. Autosomal recessive

109. Which of the following speech-language symptoms is NOT associated with Fragile X syndrome?
    a. Self-talk
    b. Perseveration
    c. Cluttered speech
    d. All these symptoms

110. Of the following congenital syndromes that can cause speech-language problems, which one is classified as a chromosomal syndrome?
    a. Hurler syndrome
    b. Hunter syndrome
    c. Turner syndrome
    d. Phenylketonuria

111. According to ASHA's Code of Ethics, which of the following SLP behaviors regarding client prognoses would be ethical?
  a. To tell clients and family it is impossible to give a prognosis because SLP is too complicated.
  b. To give clients and family members some general idea about prognosis after evaluation.
  c. To tell clients and family giving a prognosis is unethical by guaranteeing therapy results.
  d. To give clients and family a prognosis only with standardized test results on the disorder.

112. Regarding referrals, which of the following actions by the SLP would be acceptable in view of the ASHA Code of Ethics?
  a. To refer a client to another professional or agency based on the client's best interest
  b. To refer a client to another professional or agency based on the SLP's financial interest
  c. To refer a client to another professional or agency based on the SLP's personal interest
  d. To give a client services based only on a referral from a personal or professional source

113. According to ASHA, which of the following is true of ethical behavior by a supervising SLP?
  a. It is the responsibility of the supervisee to keep from violating the ASHA Code of Ethics.
  b. It is the supervisor's responsibility to keep supervisees from violating the Code of Ethics.
  c. If a supervisor delegates service tasks, delegated staff are responsible for client welfare.
  d. It is acceptable if supervisors delegate professional tasks to nonprofessional supervisees.

114. You are the SLP with the task of selecting test materials to evaluate a client with severe aphasia. Which of the following would be MOST appropriate?
  a. A standardized, norm-referenced assessment instrument
  b. A nonstandardized, criterion-referenced test instrument
  c. A standardized or nonstandardized, criterion-referenced test
  d. A standardized, norm-referenced or criterion-referenced test

115. You have a software program that analyzes test instruments for reliability. You use it to see how well the items on a norm-referenced test correlate with each other. This measure is an example of which type of reliability?
  a. Test-retest reliability
  b. Parallel forms reliability
  c. Decision consistency reliability
  d. Internal consistency reliability

116. Of the following experimental research designs, which one is a complex design?
  a. Factorial
  b. Within-subjects
  c. Pretest-posttest
  d. Between-subjects

117. To adhere to the principles of test construction, what is true about what the manual for a standardized test should include?
  a. There is no need for the authors to offer their rationale for the test.
  b. Which qualifications are required of examiners should be identified.
  c. Making a description of how the test was developed is unnecessary.
  d. Only administering, scoring, and interpreting directions are needed.

118. According to NCEO tracking and analysis for more than 20 years of state educational policies and practices in making accommodations for students with disabilities in testing and learning, which MOST accurately reflects their findings?
    a. Because the IDEA mandating accommodations is a federal law, they are uniform across states.
    b. There is a significant amount of variation in accommodation decisions among the U.S. states.
    c. There is significant variation in accommodation decisions among and even within the states.
    d. There is significant variation in these decisions among and within states and among schools.

119. Which of the following is accurate regarding provisions of the NCLB Act (2001)?
    a. States but not individual schools are more accountable.
    b. Local use of federal education funds has stricter rules.
    c. Parents are to be more involved in children's education.
    d. Federal, not state, standards qualify states for funding.

120. When a state Department of Education (DOE) awards a grant to a school district to issue scholarship funds to an employee pursuing a SLP degree, which of the following is LEAST likely to be a report that the scholarship recipient would be required to provide annually to the DOE?
    a. A copy of the recipient's course grade reports to date in the degree program
    b. A copy of a clinical report on a client evaluation that the recipient has written
    c. A copy, signed and dated, of the updated agreement for the scholarship funds
    d. A copy of a mentoring or supervision report completed by the mentor or supervisor

Answers and Explanations

1. C: Between the ages of 1 and 2 years, children typically can point to a few of their own body parts when they are asked. From 4 to 6 months of age (A), babies look in the direction of sounds, react to changes in parents' vocal tones, and notice sound-making toys and music. From 7 months to 1 year (B), they typically listen when spoken to, recognize nouns naming common things (e.g., *shoe, cup, juice, book*) and start to respond to spoken requests like "Come here" but cannot yet point to body parts. From 2 to 3 years (D), children typically can follow two-step directions (e.g., "Get your shirt, and put it in the hamper"), understand opposite meanings like *big/little* and *stop/go*, and enjoy listening to extended stories as well as point to their body parts on request.

2. B: Semantics is the domain of language involving the meanings of words. To understand and ask "Why" questions involve meaning. Phonology (A) is the domain involving speech sounds and their organization and relationships. Syntax (C) is the domain involving the arrangement of words into phrases, clauses, and sentences. Pragmatics (D) is the domain involving the use of language within social contexts, including its effects on others.

3. A: A 1-year-old's typical response to another person's distress of also showing distress or crying indicates social skills development as it indicates the child's relationship and reaction to others. Motor skills (B) development typical of 1-year-olds includes pulling up on furniture to stand, cruising (stepping while holding onto furniture), and picking up small objects with thumb and forefinger. Cognitive skills (C) development at this age includes seeing and then crawling toward toys and similar attempts to accomplish simple objectives. Language skills (D) development typical at this age includes understanding simple spoken directions and saying the first word.

4. D: The SVO word order is used by the most speakers of different world languages (including Albanian, Greek, all Germanic and Romance languages, etc.). The SOV (A) word order is used in the largest number of *languages* (including Turkish, Hungarian, Armenian, Korean, Japanese, Burmese, Basque, Hindi, Bengali, etc.) rather than of speakers. The VSO (B) word order is preferred in Arabic, Hebrew, Irish, Gaelic, Welsh, and others. The VOS (C) word order is used in only a few languages, including Northwest American and Canadian Indian tribal languages. (Note: English, like Russian and Latin, allows varying word orders.)

5. A: Phonetics is the branch of linguistics dealing mainly with how we produce and perceive speech sounds, their properties, and how we describe or represent them. Phonology (B) is the branch dealing with any given language's system of speech sounds, the rules of that system, and the patterns and relationships of speech sounds. Phonemics (C) deals with the study, development, classification, interrelations, and changes in the phonemes (= speech sounds) of any given languages. Therefore, (D) is incorrect.

6. B: Cognitive theories of phonological acquisition hold that children are active learners in the process of developing phonological awareness and skills. Conversely, Universalist-Linguistic theories hold that children are passive learners. A linear sequence of phonological development (A) is a principle of Universalist-Linguistic theories; cognitive theories posit nonlinear phonological development. That all children's phonological development following the same order and manner (C) is a belief of Universalist-Linguistic theories, while cognitive theories believe children's phonological development does include individual differences (D).

7. C: The genitive case of the English pronoun is the possessive case. The accusative (A), or objective, pronoun case in English indicates that the pronoun is the object of the verb. The nominative (B), or subjective, pronoun case in English indicates that the pronoun is the subject of the sentence or clause. The ablative (D) case is used in Latin to mean by, with, or from, but no longer exists in English, having been replaced by those prepositions, one of which will precede an object separately rather than inflecting the object word itself.

8. D: Operant conditioning is included in learning theories of language development, which are based in behaviorism. When the parents give the child spaghetti after he or she repeats the correct pronunciation, they are selectively reinforcing (rewarding) the desired behavior. Classical conditioning (A) is also a learning theory but involves conditioning via association. For example, if the parents say "spaghetti" every time they serve it, eventually, the child responds the same way to hearing the word alone as to the food. Another learning theory is social learning theory (B), which states children need not receive reinforcements directly but learn from observing and then imitating models like their parents (and observing others being rewarded for certain behaviors and then imitating these). Generative grammar (C) is NOT a learning theory: It is a feature of nativist theories like that of Noam Chomsky, which propose children have innate abilities, like a Language Acquisition Device (LAD) and a Universal Grammar, for developing language rather than learning language via interactions with the environment, as learning theories propose.

9. C: Positive behavioral support programs emphasize prevention by giving all students positive reinforcement and other supports for desired behaviors. These are found to avert many behavior problems at the lower tiers, thus (A) is incorrect. Educators introduce intervention as needed in the middle tier(s) and provide progressively more intensive intervention to the highest tier, thus (B) is incorrect. It is not true that such programs eschew punishment (D): This and other aversive consequences for undesirable behaviors may be introduced as well as using positive reinforcement for desirable behaviors.

10. B: Albert Bandura stated in his Social Learning Theory that people learn by observing others' modeling behaviors and then imitating them. Unlike Skinner's (C) behaviorist theory, which states learning equals a permanent behavioral change, Bandura maintains people may learn new information without exhibiting new behaviors. Bandura finds the conditions or steps required for learning are attention, that is, attending to the modeled behavior; retention, that is, the ability to retain and store observational information; reproduction, that is, practicing and successfully imitating the behavior; and having motivation to imitate the modeled behavior. Piaget (A) maintained that children go through progressive stages of cognitive ability and cannot learn certain concepts until they are developmentally ready to understand them. Vygotsky (D), in his sociocultural theory of learning, emphasized social interactions as the contexts for reciprocal learning and teaching, including the Zone of Proximal Development (wherein a child can do tasks with help that he or she cannot yet do alone) and the concept of scaffolding (a term coined by Jerome Bruner), that is, temporary, gradually withdrawn support.

11. A: It has often been observed that young children apply rules for regular verbs to irregular verbs, for example, "I goed yesterday" instead of "went," even though adults commonly use irregular verb tenses correctly; therefore, children are not learning this from imitating adult models, so this provides an argument against the behaviorist theory that language is learned through the conditioning processes of imitation, association, and reinforcement. Children's rate of acquiring language is too rapid to be consistent with these processes (B). Children can potentially generate an infinite number of original sentences in a language, which they could not learn through imitating models (C). Also, adults do NOT consistently correct young children's syntax (D) as they

learn language; yet, children develop language skills regardless, an argument against the behaviorist theory. If adults did constantly correct children's syntax, as in this answer choice, it would support the behaviorist view.

12. B: When children start school with language deficits, these deficits infringe on their ability to learn, to be empowered personally, to communicate with others both verbally and nonverbally, and on their developing social relationships. It is not true that families cause language deficits by preferring reading about news and current affairs over literature (A). While it is preferable for families to expose their children to reading of both kinds of materials, a family's emphasis on any kind of reading is more beneficial than its lack. While language deficits often cause children to perform below ability on school assessments, such test results do NOT reflect true intelligence deficits (C); rather, assessors may wrongly attribute such substandard performance to lower intelligence when it is really due to lower language skills. It is also NOT true that children's language development is not influenced by how much or how little their peers value reading (D): Peer groups have great influence on children, including the relative importance they accord to reading.

13. C: This expression reflects the dialect of the Amish people, a subcategory of Mennonites descended from Swiss and Alsatian Anabaptists who followed Jakob Ammann (hence the name Amish). The English spoken by the Amish is influenced by their German-speaking ancestry and preserved by their insular communities. The expression is not familial (A) because it is not specific to one family but common to the Amish as a group. It is not idiolectal (B), that is, specific to one individual's speech. It is not regional (D) because the Amish do not live exclusively in a region of Pennsylvania or even the whole state; there are also substantial Amish populations residing in Ohio, Indiana, New York State, and Canada, especially Ontario.

14. D: Students learning English as a foreign language frequently transfer incompatible properties and rules of their native languages to English. This is one example. The Chinese language does not add plural endings the way the English language does, so native Chinese speakers often leave off the –s in plural English words. While being unfamiliar with English (A) contributes to this error, the error is not *most* due to it: Lack of familiarity alone would produce more random types of errors, while transfer from the native language confers the specific error type described. The error is not due to a language disorder (B), which would produce a variety of errors rather than this specific one. Tina's error is not idiolectal (C) as it is not individual to her; it is a very common error among Chinese-speaking people when they learn English.

15. C: In Asian and Hispanic cultures, as well as Middle Eastern and Native American cultures, people find it rude or disrespectful to make direct eye contact when talking with others. Therefore, (A) is not true. This attitude contrasts with Western mainstream cultures, which teach us that, when talking to people we should "look them in the eye." Contrary to the value Western cultures place on people's admiring and complimenting their babies as beautiful or cute, Vietnamese and Hmong cultures avoid such behavior (B) because they fear that a spirit overhearing the compliments will try to steal or harm the baby. And, while American cultures view patting children on the head as affectionate or friendly, Asian cultures do not (D): They believe the head is a sacred body part that should not be touched by others.

16. C: *Co-articulation* means the phonemes in the words we speak are influenced by nearby phonemes. This makes them both variable and difficult to isolate or segment. Co-articulation is responsible for the evolution of "inpossible" to "impossible": The bilabial articulation of /p/ influenced the consonant /n/ to become the bilabial /m/. Co-articulation prevents phonemes from

being linear in production (A). It also keeps spoken phonemes from being invariant, that is, each one having only a single waveform representation (B). While we visually perceive colors on a continuum (e.g., we see red-orange between red and orange, blue-violet between blue and violet, etc.), we do NOT aurally perceive sounds on a continuum (D): We hear a syllable as *either* /pa/ *or* /ba/ but not as something in between because the two have different voice onset times (VOTs). Our separation of such different sounds facilitates our comprehension of speech and is known as *categorical perception*.

17. B: Our brains process language primarily in the left hemisphere of the brain, while music is processed primarily in the right hemisphere. Therefore, all of the sounds we hear and produce—which include both language and music—are NOT processed in the same brain hemisphere (A). Spatial information is processed mainly in the right hemisphere, while math is processed mainly in the left, so these are not both in the same hemisphere (C). The left hemisphere of the brain is responsible for analytical functions, while the right hemisphere is responsible for creative functions, not vice versa (D).

18. A: Sound waves are mechanical rather than electromagnetic, like light waves. Mechanical waves can be either longitudinal or transverse. In longitudinal waves, the particles move back and forth along the line of the wave's travel; in transverse waves, the particles move at right angles to the wave's line of travel, like ocean waves. Sound waves are always longitudinal, never transverse (B). Sound waves may be simple, that is, sinusoidal (C) or sine waves, or complex (D) waves, that is, waves made up of combinations of different frequencies and amplitudes of sine waves. Thus, sound waves are not always sinusoidal or always complex but may be either.

19. B: The ossicles (meaning "tiny bones") consist of the malleus (or hammer), incus (or anvil), and stapes (or stirrup) and are located in the middle ear. The pinna (A) (meaning "feather"), or auricle, is the visible ear structure on the outside of the head in humans. It collects and funnels sound waves. These waves pass through the ear canal (C) or external auditory meatus. When the sound waves reach the middle ear, the ossicles function to amplify and transmit them to the inner ear (D), where the hair cells in the cochlea convert them from acoustical energy to electrical energy, which is then transmitted via the auditory or acoustic nerve to the brain. Sound sensations are interpreted by the brain's auditory cortex to become sound perceptions.

20. D: The prefrontal cortex is responsible for cognitive functions like attention, planning, reasoning, and judgment, which are necessary to developing language. Neural connections in the prefrontal cortex develop throughout childhood, only attaining maturity following adolescence. Broca's area (A), which is necessary for producing speech, attains maturity in its number of neural connections around the age of 6 to 8 years. This can explain why it is normal if children do not necessarily articulate more difficult phonemes (e.g. /r/, /s/) before this age range, which is, hence, the age norm for these phonemes. Wernicke's area (B), which is necessary for understanding spoken language one hears, normally reaches maturity in its neural connections by the age of 1 year. The hippocampus (C), which is necessary for memory retention, word retrieval, and working memory, which are used in processing language, develops following birth, primarily during the child's second year.

21. A: Phonological disorders are *language* disorders that affect the *phonemic* level, entailing *cognitive* (thinking or/brain) functions that organize speech sounds into contrasting patterns, so they can be differentiated to understand and produce understandable speech. Articulation disorders are *speech* disorders that affect the *phonetic* level, entailing *motor* functions that enable correctly producing the vowel and consonant sounds of speech correctly. (Note: Many people, even

- 65 -

including SLPs, use the terms *phonological disorder* and *articulation disorder* interchangeably or incorrectly.)

22. B: Down syndrome individuals typically have physiological differences produced by the extra chromosome found in this genetic syndrome. These include short stature; short, thick fingers; Asian-appearing eyes; and a thick, protruding tongue (and sometimes an additional problem with tongue thrust). Unclear articulation, particularly with sounds involving the tongue like /s/, is caused primarily by oral characteristics of Down syndrome, not lower intelligence (A)—Down syndrome includes all levels, from profound mental impairment to normal IQ scores and any other level in the range. Behavioral problems (C) do not account for typical Down syndrome articulatory distortions. The etiology of these is not unknown (D).

23. C: Deaf and hard-of-hearing (HOH) individuals can learn to produce vocalized (voiced) speech sounds more easily because even the deaf can feel the vibrations, and the hard-of-hearing can hear some of the sound. Hence, they rely not only on visual information (A) but also on vibrations and residual hearing in those who have it. Devocalized (unvoiced) sounds are harder, not easier, to learn (C) for those with hearing loss because the HOH have less information without sound and the deaf have less information without vocal vibration. Thus, (D) is incorrect. The most successful speakers having hearing loss use a combination of all information available (auditory/sound, tactile/vibration, and visual/speech reading).

24. D: All types of dysarthrias can include hypernasal speech resonance as a characteristic; in many types, it always occurs, and in some, it is sometimes present. Cleft palate (B) typically always causes hypernasality due to the palatal opening between the mouth and nose. Speech apraxia (C), which causes difficulty with coordinating speech movements, can cause inconsistent nasality but not consistent hypernasality throughout the speech, as (A) and (B) do.

25. A: Approximately 60 percent of children referred to SLPs for help with their speech have speech sound disorders attributed to genetically based linguistic processing deficits. Hence, they are not in the minority of those referred (B). Those with genetic speech motor control deficits comprise only about 10 percent of those referred, so those with genetic language-processing deficits are a much larger group, not much smaller (C). Those with conductive hearing losses comprise a group roughly half the size of the group with genetically based language-processing deficits (about 30 percent), so (D) is also incorrect.

26. D: Some dialects in England are characterized by pronouncing words with initial /θ/ (unvoiced "th") as /f/. It is rather common to hear people from England who speak these dialects to substitute /f/ for /θ/. This is NOT an articulation disorder (A), phonological disorder (B), or language disorder (C) to be remediated. It is a normal characteristic of certain regional dialects.

27. C: Part of the definition of what are called *functional speech disorders, articulation disorders,* or *functional articulation disorders* is that their exact etiology (cause) is usually unknown. Functional speech or articulation disorders typically involve difficulty with producing one or a few speech sounds and are more often mild than severe (A). *Idiopathic* means of unknown origin, not specific to a particular child (B). Functional speech disorders are, by definition, distinctly different from phonological disorders (D).

28. D: Phonological process disorders are characterized not by errors in isolated speech sounds (A) but by patterns in speech sound production errors (B). For example, someone might consistently substitute all front consonants for back consonants, saying "beep" for *beak* and "tick" for *kick*.

- 66 -

Another error pattern characteristic of phonological process disorders is to leave out one of the consonants in a word-initial consonant cluster, for example, "poon" for *spoon* or "boke" for *broke*. Although this is developmentally normal in young children, a child who continues to omit parts of consonant clusters beyond the age norm for correct production may have a phonological process disorder.

29. A: The phonological process of substituting the stop /t/ for the fricative /f/ normally ends around the age of 3 years. The phonological process of substituting the stop /b/ for the fricative /v/ (B) normally stops around the age of 3½ years. The phonological process of substituting the stop /d/ for the affricate /dʒ/ ("j") normally disappears around the age of 4½ years. The phonological process of substituting the stop /t/ for the fricative /θ/ (unvoiced "th") normally is gone by around the age of 5 years.

30. B: According to experts, by the time a child is around 24 months old, the child's parents should be able to understand 50 to 75 percent% of the child's speech. By the age of around 18 months (A), the parents should be able to understand 25 percent of the child's speech. By the time the child is about 36 months old (C), the parents should be able to understand 75 to 100 percent of the child's speech. These approximate age norms for intelligibility to parents differ from the norms for the child's speech being intelligible to strangers: c. 25 percent by 12 months old; c. 50 percent by 24 months old; c. 75 percent by 36 months old; and 100 percent by the age of 48 months (D).

31. C: Research finds that more than 10 percent of all speech problems are caused by varying degrees of hearing loss, including mild losses. Choice (A) represents a proportion much greater than the reality. Choices (B) and (D) represent proportions lower than the fact.

32. D: *Ankyloglossia* (from the Greek for "crooked tongue") is the clinical term for "tongue-tied." It is usually caused by an abnormally short frenulum, the piece of tissue connecting the tongue to the bottom of the oral cavity. Depending on its severity, it can cause articulation problems. *Glossolalia* (A) (from the Greek for "tongue babble") is the clinical term for speech composed of unintelligible syllables that sound like speech but are meaningless. It can be a symptom of schizophrenia. It also describes the "speaking in tongues" of some religious groups. *Microglossia* (B) (from the Greek for "small tongue") is an abnormally small tongue, a congenital deformity. *Macroglossia* (C) (from the Greek for "large tongue") is an abnormally large tongue, characteristic of Down syndrome and Beckwith-Wiedemann syndrome, and can also be secondary to hypothyroidism, amyloidosis, and acromegaly.

33. C: Children begin to combine two words into meaningful expressions during the two-word stage, typically around the ages of 20 to 30 months. At 12 to 19 months (A), they are normally in the early one-word stage and only produce protowords, that is, early vocalizations that approximate adult words in sound but are consistently used to represent the same things. At 14 to 24 months (B), children are normally in the later one-word stage, wherein they utter single words that more closely resemble adult words. At 28 to 42 months (D), children are typically in the three-word stage, wherein they can combine three words in one utterance and begin to incorporate pronouns and articles.

34. B: In the stage of complex utterances (c. 48–60 months), children regularly produce utterances longer than six words. However, even though the examples given are each three words long, this does NOT mean they belong in the three-word stage (A) because they also include the use of contractions (can't and it's); the use of future concepts (tomorrow); and the use of more difficult

preposition concepts (behind)—all of which develop in the complex utterances stage and are not even typical in the four-word stage (C). Therefore (D) is incorrect.

35. A: Apraxia is predominantly localized to damage in Broca's area in the frontal lobe of the brain's left hemisphere. It is also possible that damage in the left parietal lobe may sometimes cause apraxia. Dysarthrias (B), which have at least six different types (spastic, flaccid, ataxic, hyperkinetic, hypokinetic, or mixed), are localized differently depending on type and can originate from damage to the upper motor neuron system, the lower motor neuron system, the extrapyramidal system, or any combination of these regions. Therefore, (C) and (D) are incorrect.

36. A: In some studies, researchers have found that, when they followed up with children aged 1½ to 2½ who talked later than normal, those whose receptive language skills were normal for their ages a year later were just "late bloomers" rather than having real language delays. Researchers have also found that late-talking children who use *more* gestures, not fewer (B), are more likely to catch up to age norms in verbal communication. Studies show that poorer prognoses are associated with *later* ages of diagnosis rather than earlier (C). Also, investigators find that, while a child's language development may be slower than the norm, late bloomers should still be making some kind of progress at least monthly (D). Those who do not are more likely to have true language delays.

37. B: Receptive language develops sooner than expressive language. Children must understand the language they hear before they can produce their own. A normally developing 18-month-old is hence able to follow simple directions but will only utter a few words. Being able to use 25 words or more is typical of a normally developing 2-year-old. The child described therefore does not have an expressive (A) or receptive (C) language disorder. Neither does this child have delayed language development (D).

38. C: Wernicke's aphasia disrupts the brain's receptive language functions rather than the expressive ones. People with this diagnosis can speak fluently but cannot understand others' speech. (After enough time without understanding others, their speech, though fluent, can become irrelevant or less appropriate in its content due to lack of input and feedback from others.)

39. D: Broca's aphasia disrupts the brain's expressive language functions: Patients can understand what others say to them but have difficulty producing their own intelligible spoken language. Difficulty understanding others' questions (A) or statements (B) and discriminating among the speech sounds one hears (C) all indicate problems with receptive rather than expressive language.

40. D: Meta-analysis of a number of recent research studies shows that speech-language therapy is a more effective treatment for both the phonological and vocabulary components of expressive language but that it is less effective as a treatment for the syntactic component of expressive language (B) and for receptive language problems (A).

41. C: To encourage the most authentic and comprehensive remediation of language disorders, treatment should be given in as many different settings as possible, including the home, school, and clinical contexts. Early interventions for young children should be in the home rather than a clinic (A). Students should receive treatment not only in school (B), which the law mandates they are entitled to receive at no cost, but also at home, in clinics, and so on. Integrating language goals in classrooms is preferable to pulling students out for separate treatment sessions, and where pull-out programs are used, schools should transition from these to classroom integration of language goals (D).

42. B: The law requires that treatment for infants and toddlers diagnosed with language disorders include an Individualized Family Service Plan (IFSP) that identifies the specific features of the disorder, the goals of treatment, the strategies and settings to be used, and so on. For school-age children {(A), (D)} and preschoolers {(C), (D)}, the law requires that treatment include an IEP or Individualized Education Plan. These documents are similar, and both should involve the parents and family, but the IFSP reflects the fact that the families of infants and toddlers receive a different level of service because these children are not in school yet and so cannot receive services as part of the school day.

43. A: Promoting metalinguistic awareness, that is, the ability to think about language and how it is used, is most appropriate for older children, as younger children are less cognitively ready for such abstract thinking. Focusing on more functional outcomes (B) is more appropriate when treating language disorders in younger children; with older students, focusing on making that functionality more flexible is more important. While parents should be involved with school-age children's treatments, a higher level of parental involvement (C) is more necessary with younger children not yet in school. Promoting language-based social interactions (D) is more appropriate when treating younger children; with school-age children, promoting literacy achievement and connecting treatment directly with the school curriculum are more important.

44. A: The Demands and Capacities Model proposes that, when the environment's demands for fluent speech surpass the child's capacities, dysfluencies result. The child's capacities include motor skills, cognitive development, language production skills, and emotional maturity. This theory posits that stutterers have deficits in one or more of these capacities, so the possible causes are numerous. The Covert Repair Hypothesis (B) proposes that children with inadequate phonological encoding skills develop abnormal phonetic speech plans, and their dysfluencies are normal attempts to repair these plans, so it attributes a phonological or phonetic cause. The Psychological Theory (C) attributes stuttering to a neurotic origin, finding it a symptom of internal conflicts. The Diagnostic Theory (D) attributes stuttering to a behavioral origin, that is, a learned response to parental reactions to young children's normal dysfluencies.

45. B: Neurological etiologies for stuttering are supported by research findings that four times as many boys as girls have this speech disorder (A); that twins more often stutter (C); and that more left-handed people stutter than right-handed people (D). These all suggest an association of stuttering with genetic factors. The fact that young children's cognitive development outpaces their motor skills development supports the argument for neurological causes, and the fact that boys' neurological development is slower than girls' is consistent with the fact that far more boys than girls stutter. However, the fact that some children still have persistent stuttering above the age of 6 years (B), when both sexes' motor skills should have caught up with their cognitive development, tends to refute a primarily neurological basis for stuttering.

46. C: How natural the individual's speech does or does not sound can be quite obvious, both to the SLP and to untrained listeners, and can be rated on a point scale; however, ultimately, this judgment is the most subjective of the choices. The frequency (A) and duration (B) of stuttering and the rate of speech (D) can all be objectively measured because these all involve counting—that is, the number of dysfluencies, the number of seconds in the length of dysfluencies, and the number of syllables or words in a speech sample.

47. D: Increasing pauses during turn-taking exercises or conversational speech is an example of a direct therapeutic method for treating stuttering. Changing the stutterer's environment (A) is an

- 69 -

example of an indirect therapeutic method. Modifying the speech patterns of the stutterer's parents (B) is an example of changing the stutterer's environment and, hence, is also an indirect treatment method. Focusing on the stutterer's feelings (C), attitudes, and the pragmatics of the stutterer's everyday speech are characteristic of indirect treatment methods.

48. C: Fluency shaping focuses on the stutterer's dysfluent speech and on changing it gradually through behavioral shaping. This includes incremental steps to increase the complexity (C) or length of the client's utterances from one syllable or word to conversational speech. Desensitizing the client from unpleasant emotions about stuttering (A), decreasing the stutterer's anxiety and speech avoidance behaviors (B), and increasing the stutterer's self-confidence and sense of self-worth (D) are all characteristics of the stuttering modification technique.

49. B: Although some dysfluencies are normal in young children's speech and often resolve without any treatment, ASHA advises that, if parents have concerns about their child's fluency, they should have the child tested by an SLP. Early detection and intervention can prevent true stuttering from progressing as well as giving parents peace of mind. ASHA also recommends that parents NOT interrupt young children when they are speaking (A) and that they DO give young children as much time as they need to say something (C). Parents should NOT constantly correct all of young children's normal, occasional dysfluencies (D); this can back fire, making them self-conscious about their speech and hence more prone to dysfluency.

50. A: Cul-de-sac resonance, appropriately named like a street closed at one end or a blind diverticulum or pouch in the body, results when vocal sound can resonate in the nasal cavity or pharynx but cannot be released because of some obstruction. A hypernasal (B) voice is characterized by too much speech sound resonating in the nose due to factors like cleft palate or a large velopharyngeal opening, while a hyponasal (C) voice is characterized by too little nasal resonance, usually due to upper airway blockage. The correct term for a complete absence of any nasal resonance (D) is *denasality*.

51. B: When there is a blockage of the air stream somewhere, and the obstructed form of nasal air emission occurs during speech, it makes a high-frequency, high-intensity sound. In the unobstructed (= no blockage) form, nasal air emission has a high-frequency, *low*-intensity sound, which does NOT occur in both forms (C)—and hence does NOT occur in the obstructed form (D). In other words, in both forms, the air emission has a high perceived pitch, but it sounds louder in the obstructed form and softer in the unobstructed form.

52. D: Any kind of nasopharyngeal obstruction (A), for example, enlarged adenoids, can cause mixed nasality in speech (defined as hypernasal oral consonants and hyponasal nasal consonants), as can any type of velopharyngeal dysfunction (B), and the neurological condition of apraxia (C), which can be congenital or acquired and compromises the brain's programming of motor movements for speech.

53. C: Multi-view videofluoroscopy (MVF) gives 3-D imaging of the velopharyngeal port by taking lateral, frontal (anterior-to-posterior or AP), and base or Townes' views. It also allows direct measurements. This test therefore can identify velar length and thickness. Aerodynamic testing (A) measures airflow and air pressure during phonation and can help to estimate the size of the velopharyngeal opening during phonation; however, it does not actually measure the size and thickness of the velum itself. Nasopharyngoscopy (B) uses an endoscope to view and photograph the velopharyngeal port and the velum's nasal surface during phonation. It does not, however, indicate the length and thickness of the velum. Nasometry (D) analyzes acoustic energy emitted

through the nasal and oral cavities during phonation; the ratio of the two equals *nasalance,* the acoustic measure of what we perceive as nasality. It does not measure velar length and thickness.

54. B: Velopharyngeal mislearning is a cause of phoneme-specific velopharyngeal incompetence: The individual's articulation of certain phonemes is incorrectly pharyngealized or nasalized, causing primarily hypernasal, not hyponasal (C), speech or causing nasal air emission specific to certain phonemes—especially sibilants like /s/. Articulation is often mislearned by individuals with hearing loss (A) due to deficient auditory input, particularly with sibilants, which are harder to hear and see. Velopharyngeal mislearning is always treated by speech therapy but never by surgery (D), as it is not caused by any defect of the speech structures.

55. A: The palatal lift is a prosthetic device that raises the velum in cases of inadequate velar mobility. It is helpful in cases of velopharyngeal incompetence, which is caused by physiological defects, such as neurological conditions like dysarthria and apraxia, neuromuscular disorders like myasthenia gravis, hypotonia (= weak muscle tone), and other problems with muscle function. The palatal obturator (B) is a prosthetic device used to close an open cleft or fistula of the palate. The speech bulb obturator (C) is a prosthetic device used to close the nasopharynx, which typically applies to velopharyngeal insufficiency (due to an anatomical defect rather than velopharyngeal incompetence due to a physiological defect). Prostheses do not permanently correct these problems as surgery can, but they DO work (D) to improve them in cases where surgery is contraindicated or as temporary measures.

56. B: Patients with vocal cord nodules or polyps (these are two distinct conditions whose etiologies may differ but their symptoms are similar) often experience a sensation of pain shooting from one ear to the other. Their voices are most likely to sound hoarse (A). Another common symptom is fatigue of both the voice and the body (C). It is also common for patients with these voice disorders to have voices that sound breathy, rough, harsh, or scratchy and to have a reduction of their normal pitch ranges (D); that is, they cannot produce pitches as high and as low as they could before the nodules or polyps developed.

57. C: People who learn esophageal speech (typically following laryngectomy) well enough are found to have speech that is clearest to the general listener. Buccal speech (A) or "Donald Duck speech," which uses the cheek and jaw to create air pockets, and pharyngeal speech (B), which produces the air supply in the pharynx, are also used by some, but neither is as clear as esophageal speech and consequently not used as often. Because (C) is correct, (D) is incorrect.

58. D: When a patient has just undergone laryngectomy for laryngeal cancer (the most common reason) and has no voice, an electrolarynx can provide an immediate means of producing understandable speech. This is its clearest advantage over esophageal speech, which must be learned and can take considerable time to master. The electrolarynx can be a great benefit even for temporary use, while the laryngectomee is learning esophageal speech. The robotic sound of the electrolarynx (A) is generally considered more a disadvantage than an advantage. The tracheo-esophageal puncture and other surgical procedures enable in-dwelling prosthetic voice devices as alternatives to having to hold an external device in one hand (B). The electrolarynx does not produce clearer sound than esophageal speech (C). While the former produces sound electrically and the latter uses the esophagus instead of the larynx to vibrate air, with both methods, the speaker uses his or her own articulators to shape speech sounds. The only difference is the sound quality of the vibration, not the articulations.

59. A: Broca's aphasia is caused by damage to the parts of the brain responsible for producing expressive language. Patients with Broca's aphasia have difficulty retrieving words they know, organizing their thoughts, constructing complete spoken or written sentences, getting their words in the right order for syntactic conventions, and using conventional grammatical forms. If this patient had Wernicke's aphasia (B), she would not have these problems expressing herself; she would have difficulty understanding what she heard others say instead. If she had global aphasia (C), she would have difficulty with both expressive and receptive language. If she had no aphasia (D), she would not demonstrate the expressive difficulties described.

60. B: Patients with damage to the right hemisphere of the brain are more likely to experience problems in addition to those with speech and language than are patients with damage to the left (A) hemisphere. Therefore, (C) and (D) are incorrect.

61. C: Most aphasia patients, who more often have mixed damage to both receptive and expressive language functions than purely receptive (Wernicke's) or purely expressive (Broca's) aphasia, typically have more difficulty with reading and writing printed language than they do with speaking and understanding spoken language. (A) describes expressive and receptive language problems but only with spoken language; (B) describes spoken and printed language but only expressive problems; and (D) describes both printed and spoken language but only receptive problems.

62. D: Of the progressive motor neuron diseases named, only ALS (Lou Gehrig's disease) causes degeneration in both the upper and lower motor neurons. PBP (A) causes degeneration of only lower motor neurons—specifically the bulbar motor nuclei—not of upper motor neurons. SMA (B) causes deterioration of the spinal anterior horn cells, roots, and nerves—all lower motor neurons, not upper motor neurons. PLS (C) causes deterioration of only upper motor neurons—specifically the motor cells in the cortex and the corticobulbar and corticospinal tracts—not of lower motor neurons.

63. A: On the ALS Severity Scale, at the mildest level, a patient swallows normally, progressing to some abnormalities; to minor difficulties with swallowing; to taking smaller bites and longer times to chew and swallow; to requiring a diet of only soft foods; to requiring a diet of only liquids; to needing a liquid diet supplemented with tube feedings (C); to requiring mostly tube feeding with only occasional liquefied foods by mouth; to not being able to take any nourishment by mouth (D); to needing medications to reduce mucosal, salivary, and other secretions or having secretions suctioned out (B) due to inability to swallow them; to ultimately aspirating these secretions, that is, inhaling them through the airways into the lungs instead of swallowing them through the esophagus into the stomach. Aspiration is very dangerous: It can cause pneumonia or death.

64. B: According to the research, there is no evidence that exercising helps dysarthria symptoms in ALS patients, and there is even some evidence that it can harm them. Therefore, such patients who can still speak should be advised to conserve their remaining energy. These patients should also be encouraged to speak at a slow rate (A) consistently, to exaggerate their articulation (C) of speech sounds and articulate them as precisely as possible, and to consider introducing the use of amplifiers (D) to make their speech louder so others can hear and understand them better.

65. C: The ataxic type of dysarthria, characterized by incoordination of the speech movements, is caused by neurological damage localized to the cerebellar control circuit. The flaccid (A) type of dysarthria, characterized by weakness of the speech movements, is caused by neurological damage localized to the lower motor neurons. The spastic (B) type of dysarthria, characterized by spasticity or hypertonicity of the speech movements, is caused by neurological damage localized to the upper

motor neurons. The hypokinetic (D) type of dysarthria, characterized by rigidity of speech movements and problems with scaling speech movements, is caused by neurological damage localized to the basal ganglia control circuit.

66. D: Apraxia of speech is caused by neurological damage localized to the brain's left hemisphere. Neurological damage localized to the basal ganglia control circuit (A) does not cause speech apraxia but does cause the hypokinetic and hyperkinetic types of dysarthria, characterized respectively by rigid or involuntary speech movements. Neurological damage localized to the cerebellar control circuit (B) also does not cause apraxia but does cause the ataxic type of dysarthria, characterized by uncoordinated speech movements. Neurological damage localized to the brain's right hemisphere (C) does not cause motor speech disorders (apraxia or dysarthrias) but can cause receptive aphasia (a language disorder) and other symptoms in addition to language problems.

67. C: Apraxia of speech involves damage in the brain's right hemisphere to the areas responsible for programming and planning the correct types and sequences of motor movements of speech. The brain's coordination of motor speech movements (A) is damaged in the ataxic type of dysarthria. The brain's control of the muscle movements of speech (B) is damaged in the hyperkinetic type of dysarthria, symptomatized by involuntary movements. The brain's control of the muscular strength of speech movements (D) is damaged in the flaccid type of dysarthria, symptomatized by weakness. The dysarthrias involve various aspects of the brain's control over the movement of speech muscles, while apraxia involves the brain's programming and planning of speech movements.

68. B: According to the Centers for Disease Control and Prevention (CDC, 2010, 2012), children from the ages of birth to 4 years, adolescents from the ages of 15 to 19 years, and adults aged 65 years and older are the age groups found most likely to incur traumatic brain injuries (TBIs).

69. A: One characteristic of individuals with cognitive communication disorders is that their speech remains fluent, and they retain the ability to use the meanings and structures of language correctly. This often makes language assessment batteries designed with aphasia patients in mind unsuitable for cognitive communication-disordered patients, as these tests do not evaluate conversation and thus will not reveal the true extent of the problem, which includes impairment in the ability to organize their thoughts, respond to what others say focusing on the main point or topic, and take turns in conversations (B). Cognitive communication disorders also involve difficulties with understanding and using the pragmatics of language (C), like "reading" social contexts accurately and responding appropriately, and impairment in executive functions (D), like decision making, planning, goal setting, problem solving, flexibility, self-control, self-monitoring, and self-evaluation.

70. B: Right-hemisphere neurological damage from strokes and other traumatic brain injuries can often cause symptoms of visuo-spatial neglect, cause damage to the mobility of the LEFT limbs (A), cause LEFT visual field deficits (C), and DO often cause impairment in the ability to understand figurative language (D)—that is, expressions like irony, sarcasm, jokes, puns, other wordplay; metaphors, similes, alternate meanings; and other nonliteral figures of speech and subtle nuances of language. Damage to one hemisphere typically (with some exceptions) causes problems on the opposite side of the body due to the cross-wiring of body part innervations with the opposing cranial nerves.

71. C: The Glossopharyngeal (IX) nerve controls only the stylopharyngeus muscle. The Hypoglossal (XII) nerve (A) controls six swallowing muscles—the intrinsic tongue muscles—the hyoglossus, geniohyoid, genioglossus, styloglossus, and thyrohyoid muscles. The Trigeminal (V) nerve (B) controls four swallowing muscles: the masticatory muscles—the mylohyoid, tensor veli palatini

- 73 -

muscles—and the anterior belly of the digastric muscles. The Facial (VII) nerve (D) controls three swallowing muscles: the facial and stylohyoid muscles and the posterior belly of the digastric muscles. (The Vagus [X] nerve also controls six other swallowing muscles.)

72. D: The cricopharyngeus muscle is attached from the front to the sides of the cricoid cartilage. This muscle compresses the UES against the rear of the cricoid cartilage, causing it to close. The pharynx constrictor muscles (A) are a layer of muscles on the pharynx that begin on the cranium, the hyoid bone, and the front of the thyroid cartilage. They insert onto a posterior median raphe. The submental muscles (B) begin on the mandible (lower jaw) and attach to the hyoid bone and the tongue. The pyriform recesses (C) are not muscles; they are two spaces found in the pharynx, positioned laterally to the larynx.

73. C: The normal adult human eating and swallowing processes involve more than 30 different muscles and nerves. These processes do not involve more than 40 (A), fewer than 20 (B), or fewer than 10 (D) muscles and nerves.

74. B: The four-stage model of eating and swallowing included the oral preparatory, oral propulsive, pharyngeal, and esophageal stages. These stages were described as sequential. This was adequate to represent how people swallow liquids. However, it did not address how people chew and swallow solid foods: While the stages are correct, the four-stage model did not address the fact that these stages also overlap. Hence, it was replaced with the process model, which additionally includes Stage I transport, food processing, and Stage II transport. Thus, the problem with the four-stage model was NOT the number of stages (A). Its description of the process was NOT later proven inaccurate by imaging (C). It described discrete stages rather than overlapping ones, not vice versa (D).

75. A: *Iatrogenic etiology* means the condition (in this case, dysphagia) was caused by physician or medical staff activity, including examination, testing, treatment, manner, diagnosis, and so on. Surgical resection (B) of any of the areas involved in swallowing can cause dysphagia. Dysphagia can be caused by fibrosis (scar tissue) forming as a result of radiation (C) therapy. Dysphagia can also be a side effect of some medications (D). However, introducing caustic materials (A) to the alimentary tract is not a normal medical practice, as these are known to cause tissue damage. The ingestion of caustic matter is more likely to be done accidentally or deliberately by the patient. This etiology is classified under structural lesions as caustic materials will damage the swallowing structures.

76. D: Scleroderma is a condition that causes progressive hardening and attenuation of the soft tissues, including the esophageal tissues, which narrow and harden. Scleroderma can also weaken the lower esophageal muscle, which can result in reflux (backing up of food and stomach acid into the throat and mouth) as well as weak swallowing movements. Multiple sclerosis (A) can cause dysphagia by impairing the brain areas and nerves that control muscular strength, sensation, and movement. Esophageal spasm (B) is a condition wherein the esophageal muscles suddenly tighten, which can stop food from moving into the stomach by closing the esophagus. Dermatomyositis (C) is an autoimmune disease that causes inflammation resulting in muscle weakness and pain (along with other symptoms), which can result in dysphagia.

77. B: Chemoradiation therapy to treat cancer of the head and neck can frequently cause delays in the initiation of swallowing, decreases in pharyngeal transport of food, and inadequate protection of the larynx. These are all functional impairments in swallowing. Diverticulitis (A) consists of diverticula, or pouches, forming in the walls of the digestive tract, including the esophagus or

pharynx. This cause is obstructive. Cervical osteophytes (C) are bone spurs that grow out from the cervical vertebrae and are more common in elderly patients. These can restrict the food pathway and move food toward the airway. This is also an obstructive cause. GERD (D) involves stomach acid repeatedly backing up into the esophagus, which can create esophageal ulcers. These ulcers can cause scar tissue formation, narrowing the esophagus. This is also an obstructive cause of dysphagia.

78. C: One of the impairments that leads to aspiration, most often *during* swallowing, is when the vocal folds do not close adequately, allowing material to pass through them. When liquids enter the pharynx prematurely due to not being contained by the oral cavity (A), this most often causes aspiration *before* swallowing. When the larynx does not close soon enough after a bolus reaches the larynx (B), this also causes aspiration *before* swallowing. When material accumulated in the pharynx is not all swallowed and some remains (D), this can cause aspiration *after* swallowing, when the patient resumes breathing after swallowing and inhales the leftover material.

79. A: Manometry is a test wherein a small tube is inserted into the esophagus. The tube is connected at its other end to a computer. While the patient swallows, the tube senses the pressure against it, and the computer program quantifies the amount of pressure. The clinician can then determine whether the esophagus exerts normal pressure during swallowing. Laryngoscopy (B) uses either a fiber-optic laryngoscope or a mirror to view the back of the throat for obstructions or abnormal swallowing function. pH monitoring (C) is a test that measures how frequently stomach acid enters the esophagus and how long the acid remains in the esophagus. This can help diagnose GERD. Esophagoscopy (D), or upper gastrointestinal endoscopy, inserts an endoscope (a flexible, lighted instrument) into the esophagus and sometimes the stomach and small intestine to view and photograph them. The endoscope can also be used to remove tissue for biopsy. This test can detect cancers, polyps, other growths or obstructions, and inflammation.

80. B: In some cases, an endoscope can be inserted for imaging and then also used to remove certain obstructions like polyps or foreign objects. When the obstruction cannot be removed endoscopically, it may be removed surgically. Dilation (A) can be done via inserting an endoscope and using its imaging as a guide, inserting and inflating a balloon, or inserting a bougie that gently expands narrowed parts of the esophagus. Dilation is also used to treat obstructive dysphagia. However, medication (A) is prescribed for esophageal infections (antibiotics) or esophagitis, heartburn, or GERD (antacids, acid reducers), not to remove obstructions. Exercises {(C), (D)} are prescribed to train the muscles in dysphagia with neurological, muscular, or neuromuscular origins (i.e., problems in the brain, nervous system, or muscles); they do not remove obstructions. Dietary changes (D) can make swallowing easier for dysphagia patients but will not remove obstructions.

81. C: Inserting a stent is preferable to endoscopic dilation (B) because dilation has a greater risk of perforating the esophagus in cancer patients. Botulinum toxin (A) (brand names include Botox, Myobloc, Dysport, and Xeomin) is used as a treatment for achalasia, a condition that enlarges the esophagus, impairs peristaltic contractions, and causes stiffness of the esophageal muscles and failure of the lower esophageal sphincter to relax. Just as it temporarily paralyzes facial muscles to erase wrinkles (and is sometimes used in the head to treat or prevent chronic migraines), botulinum toxin temporarily (for about 6 months) paralyzes esophageal muscles and the LES, so they relax. It does not treat cancer (and can even cause dysphagia, as a side effect in patients with neuromuscular diseases like ALS, myasthenia gravis, or Lambert-Eaton syndrome). A proton pump inhibitor (D), a medication that inhibits the formation of stomach acid, can treat dysphagia symptoms caused by digestive problems like esophagitis, heartburn, and GERD, but not cancer.

82. D: The process of audition involves reactions that are all mechanical, while the processes of vision, olfaction, gustation, and touch sensation all involve chemical reactions. The entire sequence of hearing, including the brain's processing of sensory reception, involves both voluntary and involuntary reactions rather than only one or the other {(A), (B)}.

83. C: The stapedius reflex protects our hearing from overly loud noises when the stapedius muscle pulls the eardrum and ossicles away from each other to minimize vibration, damping our hearing of the noise. Hence, it does the opposite of amplifying sound (A). This reflex does not activate the stapes (B): The malleus is activated to vibrate by the tympanic membrane (eardrum); the malleus's vibration activates the incus; the incus's vibration activates the stapes. The stapedius reflex, in addition to protecting us from loud noises, damps our hearing of our own voices, which would otherwise block out many other sounds coming from outside of us. Hence, it does not enable us to hear our own voices (D) but reduces this hearing, so we can still hear other sounds while talking.

84. B: Universal newborn hearing screening is advised by ASHA and other organizations concerned with health. Hearing loss is the most common newborn disability and has often gone undetected without newborn hearing screening. Early intervention (which depends on early detection) is found to prevent or minimize language development and learning problems due to hearing loss. The recommendation for hearing screening is not limited to babies at higher risk for hearing loss (A), such as infants in neonatal intensive care units (C), who must be screened, but encompasses all newborns. Following birth is NOT too early to screen (D) for hearing problems.

85. A: This person's hearing loss is asymmetrical; that is, it is not of the same degree or configuration in both ears. The left ear has normal hearing at the lowest frequency and moderate loss at the highest frequency, while the right ear has moderately severe loss at the lowest frequency and severe loss at the highest frequency. Hence, the loss is not unilateral (B), that is, in only one ear; both ears have hearing loss at some frequencies. The person does not have symmetrical (C) hearing loss, that is, the same in both ears, because the degree (dB level of loss) and configuration (frequencies where loss exists) are not different in each ear. The loss is not high-frequency (D) because there is also hearing loss at a low frequency.

86. B: Hearing aids amplify sounds; that is, they make them louder; whereas cochlear implants convert sounds from acoustic signals to electric signals—the same thing a normal cochlea does but which a damaged cochlea cannot do. The reverse (A) is incorrect. Neither device transmits {(C), (D)} sound: With hearing aids, the outer, middle, and inner ears still transmit the sound to the brain via the auditory nerve, while hearing aids enable a louder sound to be transmitted. Cochlear implants supplant the hair cells' function of converting sound from acoustical to electrical energy when the hair cells have been destroyed or inactivated, directly stimulating the auditory nerve in their place. Neither device sharpens {(C), (D)} the sound.

87. C: According to ASHA, the SLP will often need to counsel parents wanting advice about whether to try hearing aids (which benefit some children but not others) or ASL while awaiting cochlear implant surgery, and this is within the SLP's scope of services. Of course, deaf educators as available can counsel parents about ASL (A), but this does not mean the SLP cannot do so in addition to or in lieu of a deaf educator or ASL specialist. Counseling on this issue is not restricted to the surgeon (B). Audiologists fit and test hearing aids and can counsel parents in this case (D) but are not the only ones to help parents decide whether to use them. Families in this situation frequently look to the SLP for advice, which SLPs can give based on their experience with other families and data from published parents' reports.

88. D: Adults who did not lose their hearing until after they had developed speech and language are the best candidates for cochlear implantation. Those born deaf must first learn what sounds are through instruction. Adults who have not obtained enough benefit from using hearing aids are good candidates, whereas those hearing very well using hearing aids (A) are not advised to pursue serious surgery if it is unnecessary. Cochlear implants are considered for adults with severe to profound bilateral hearing loss rather than only moderate loss in one ear (B). Deaf adults who identify strongly with deaf culture (C) frequently refuse to consider any measures to allow them to hear better or hear at all, as they feel being deaf is not a disability and hearing would compromise their deaf identity and belonging to deaf culture.

89. B: Research studies have found that, by counseling their clients as needed, SLPs can also enhance the effectiveness of their therapy that directly addresses speech, language, and hearing impairments. Experts note that the SLP's counseling of clients is not limited to only informing, instructing, and advising (A); it moreover increases treatment efficacy and helps clients to cope with the emotional and psychosocial effects of their speech, language, or hearing impairment. Therefore, (D) is incorrect. It is important for SLPs to remember that the counseling they give their clients does NOT qualify them as psychotherapists, so their counseling does NOT take the place of such services (C). Counseling is within the SLP's scope to help clients cope with the stress of their communication disorders and adapt to the changes they cause but not to resolve all of a client's psychological problems.

90. D: Neither the parents of the child whose records are accessed nor the employees of the participating agency documenting such records access are included in the IDEA's confidentiality provision regarding record of access (§300.563). The parents and the agency employees are the only exceptions. For all other parties obtaining access to the child's education records, the agency must keep a record of the party's name, the date access was granted, and the purpose for which that party was authorized to use the child's records.

91. C: When school SLPs have been surveyed recently by researchers, they often report that the two most common ways they receive information about students' therapy from professionals at other facilities are in formal reports and via parental reports equally. Far fewer school SLPs report receiving such information via phone calls {(A), (D)}. Even fewer report receiving such information via e-mails (B).

92. D: We do not use the results of just one assessment to make a diagnosis. Interpreting research data is analogous: We cannot choose a particular intervention approach based on the results of one research study of that intervention. Just as multiple assessments are needed for diagnosis, multiple studies are needed to judge the potential effectiveness of an intervention. One study may show statistically nonsignificant or weak effects of an intervention, while another may show significant or good effects of the same intervention. Therefore, a treatment method should neither be discarded (A) nor adopted (B) based on only one study, and the results of only one study are never sufficient (C) for this decision.

93. D: In none of these practice settings is the SLP alone responsible for making the decision to terminate speech-language therapy. In Birth-to-3 programs (A), the child's third birthday is the criterion for automatic discharge. (The child's discharge planning, in which the SLP may participate, can include transitioning to a preschool program; however, discharge from the Birth-to-3 program is still automatic at age 3.) In public school systems (B), the SLP is required to comply with the IDEA, and only once the multidisciplinary team discusses the impacts of the child's communication status on the child's learning and social skills and makes a collective decision can the child be

discharged. In health care systems (C), the paying or accrediting agencies typically affect case management decisions limiting the extent of services; for example, in hospitals. While the SLP may participate in discharge planning, the patient's medical status is the ultimate criterion for discharge determination.

94. C: ASHA's criteria for discharging SLP clients include considering whether family support is available, whether treatment will be available when the client is transferred to a different facility, and other issues of treatment resource availability. ASHA criteria for discharge are found by researchers to be both client-centered and disability-centered rather than only the former but not the latter (A). ASHA discharge criteria also reflect both standardized test results and measures of functional skills rather than just the latter but not the former (B). Additionally, the ASHA discharge guidelines do include considering the impact of a communication disorder on a client's educational, vocational, emotional, or social performance in everyday life (D).

95. B: According to experts reviewing the research literature on teacher referrals of students to SLPs in public schools, to provide the best service quality possible to students, the relationships between school SLPs and teachers must be made stronger. This includes that SLPs must view teachers as vitally important to the referral process. SLPs might never evaluate some students without teacher referrals, thus (A) is incorrect. Teachers spend most of the school day with students, whereas SLPs do not have sufficient time to evaluate every student regularly; therefore, teachers may be the first to notice some student behaviors (C). Most research studies find that teachers tend NOT to over-refer students to SLPs (D) but rather that they tend to under-refer students for speech-language deficits, particularly in articulation and voice.

96. A: State EHDI coordinators cite inadequate reimbursement for diagnosis as one barrier to connecting newborns who fail hearing screenings with needed services. Other obstacles they identify to follow up include privacy regulations (B), the lack of proximity for many families to EHDI facilities (C) because there are not enough facilities, and the fact that most EHDI programs do NOT screen preschoolers' hearing (D).

97. A: ASHA bases its treatment efficacy summaries on data collected from the ASHA National Outcomes Measurement System (NOMS). According to these (2008) data, through SLP treatment, c. 80 percent patients diagnosed with aphasia secondary to left-hemisphere strokes attained one or more levels of progress on the Functional Communication Measures (FCMs—seven-level rating scales from least to most functional, measuring improvement in various clinical areas). The data find that two thirds (i.e., about 67 percent) of preschoolers diagnosed with autism spectrum disorders (B) demonstrated gains of one or more levels on the FCM for Spoken Language Production after SLP intervention. About 70 percent of preschoolers with language disorders (C) were found to gain one or more levels on the FCMs for Spoken Language Production or Spoken Language Comprehension from SLP intervention. Of adults with dysphagia who required feeding tubes (D) when SLP treatment began, about 60 percent no longer needed these and could swallow safely at the end of SLP treatment.

98. A: Improvement of less than 20 percent after 3 months is equally likely to be due to chance as to treatment. This does not indicate slow but adequate improvement (B). Inaccurate measurement is a possibility but is only one variable and not necessarily the reason for this number (C). While lack of progress beyond chance suggests that the therapy chosen is ineffective, this does not automatically mean the program should be discarded and replaced (D) with an entirely different therapy program. There are often relatively minor adjustments or changes to a therapy program that can

make a great difference in its efficacy. These should be investigated and tried before scrapping the entire program for another.

99. A: A functional magnetic resonance imaging scan (fMRI) shows images of the metabolic function of different parts of the brain. In both MRI and fMRI, the magnetic field and gradient coil of the machine use atomic physics principles for brain imaging. However, the MRI (B) scan gives 3-D pictures of the brain's anatomical structure only, whereas the fMRI scan gives pictures of the brain's metabolic function, showing which regions are more or less active during various cognitive processes. EEG (C) or electroencephalography records the brain's electrical rather than metabolic activity, showing normal or abnormal brain waves. A PET (D) or positron emission tomography scan shows relative metabolic brain activity as an fMRI does but by measuring glucose in different brain areas, whereas an fMRI measures alignment in the brain's water molecules, indicating which areas need more oxygen. The need for more glucose and more oxygen both signal greater activity. However, a key difference is that the PET scan is invasive because it requires injecting radioactive glucose into the patient, while the fMRI is noninvasive.

100. D: Many websites and software programs now exist that enable clients and students to practice their therapeutic exercises independently. This affords them control over the tasks and the ability to work at their own pace, when and where they choose, and for comfortable durations, and it gives them immediate, nonjudgmental feedback. SLPs can use the Internet to research (B) efficacy studies, evidence-based therapy practices, and so on. ASHA and other therapy-, education-, and health-focused organizations; government agencies; support groups; and many others now have good websites. Parents and family can get information on advocating (C) for their children or relatives via such websites.

101. B: Of the choices given, the SLP would first select a particular theoretical framework for intervention that he or she judges is most applicable to the client's individual communication deficits and therapeutic needs. Then, the SLP would identify which treatment methods (D) are most reflective of the theoretical model he or she has selected; critique how appropriate each of these methods is, and how effective if that information is available; and select which methods to use in therapy, providing his or her rationale for selecting certain methods over others. Then, the SLP would identify which materials (A) are most consistent with the methods he or she has selected; critique how appropriate all available materials are, and how effective if this information is available; and select the materials to use in therapy, giving his or her rationale for selecting some materials over others. Then, the SLP would consider which design and data collection methods (C) are most compatible with the theoretical framework and methods chosen and what overall kinds of efficacy data will be targeted for collection and analysis.

102. C: Experts who have designed and administered training in counseling to students preparing to become SLPs have noted that asking open (a.k.a. open-ended) questions, while harder for SLP students to master, are preferred because they allow clients and family members to respond in a variety of ways. Conversely, closed questions tend to require a specific response (B); they are only better for saving time and obtaining information, whereas open questions encourage respondents to talk more, better convey the SLP's interest, and uncover more of the respondent's feelings, perspectives, and knowledge. SLP students in counseling training have reflected that desire to appear "professional" or discomfort with silence may tempt clinicians to ask too many closed questions. The experts also note that questions are considered a secondary, not primary (A) interviewing behavior, because silence—a primary interviewing behavior—increases rather than decreases (D) client responses.

103. D: The inherent flexibility of most authentic assessments and the ability of this approach to be individualized for clients with special needs or cultural diversity are considered advantages. The fact that authentic assessments, unlike norm-referenced tests, are usually not standardized means that the assessor does not know how reliable (i.e., it can be replicated with the same or similar results across administrations and populations) and valid (i.e., it tests what it is meant to test) the assessment is (A), which is considered a disadvantage. Another disadvantage is that SLPs must be very experienced and skilled clinically to implement authentic assessments successfully (B). Additional disadvantages of authentic assessments versus standardized tests include that authentic assessments require more planning time, whereas standardized measures have already been designed and published; that authentic assessments may not be as objective as standardized tests; and in some situations, that authentic assessments may not be as practical to administer (C).

104. A: Most norm-referenced, standardized tests tend to be static by measuring what someone knows rather than dynamic by showing how one learns. This can be a disadvantage. However, an advantage of these tests is that they do NOT require extensive clinical experience and skill to administer and score (B). They include manuals with clear instructions for administration, scoring, and interpretation. While standardized, norm-referenced tests have been vetted for validity and reliability before publication, if they are not administered exactly according to the instructions, this can compromise the validity and reliability of the results. Another caveat with standardized tests comparing scores to representative sample populations is that they may be inappropriate to give to linguistically and culturally diverse students (D), whose knowledge and experience differ from those of the sample populations.

105. A: Some children with autism spectrum disorders (ASDs), intellectual disabilities (ID), and other developmental disabilities are unable to complete standardized tests. Diagnostic interventions or dynamic assessments can be used instead to assess their performance levels. These are NOT very similar to standardized, norm-referenced tests (B). They do not compare scores to sample populations' scores. They are not given uniformly to all children but are individualized. They ARE likely to use observations of the child's spontaneous communication (C) as an authentic assessment method. Due to their specialization, these kinds of assessments are likely to take MORE time to administer than standardized instruments (D).

106. B: Activities that work on developing strategies for responding to unpredictable individuals, interactions, and situations are age-appropriate for a high school or middle school student on the autism spectrum. Those with ASDs have difficulty with the unexpected and nonroutine, so helping them develop strategies can facilitate their social interaction and coping skills. Working on identifying emotions using favorite books, characters, or drawings (A) is more age-appropriate for elementary, school-age children on the autism spectrum. Working on taking turns in favorite games like Memory to prepare a child for conversational turn taking (C) is more age-appropriate for preschoolers on the autism spectrum. Working on saying or signing *more*, which is an important word in functional communication (D), is more age-appropriate for young children on the autism spectrum. For example, an adult can push the child on a swing and then stop, waiting for the child to indicate *more* or wait until the child indicates *more* before refilling his or her drink, food, or snack, and so on.

107. C: Traits that have genes located on different chromosomes are independently assorted traits. The principle of independent assortment says that pairs of alleles for different traits are inherited independently of one another. When one allele from each parent's pair is inherited (A), this reflects the genetic principle of segregation, which states that each parent's pair of alleles separate, so the offspring inherits one allele from each parent. This segregation takes place during the process of

meiosis, wherein sex cells are formed (B). According to the principle of independent assortment, inheriting one particular trait does NOT influence whether another different trait is also inherited (D) because different pairs of alleles are inherited independently.

108. D: The autosomal recessive pattern, wherein both copies of the gene in each cell are mutated, accounts for about 75 to 80 percent of nonsyndromic genetic deafness. About 20 to 25 percent of cases of nonsyndromic genetic deafness are inherited via the autosomal dominant (B) pattern, wherein only one copy of the mutated gene in each cell causes hearing loss—most often inherited from a parent with hearing loss. The X-linked pattern (C) of inheritance, wherein the mutated gene causing deafness is located on the X chromosome, accounts for c. 1 to 2 percent of cases of nonsyndromic genetic deafness. Males inheriting X-linked nonsyndromic deafness usually develop hearing loss earlier and more severely than females inheriting it. Fathers cannot pass X-linked traits to their sons. Nonsyndromic genetic deafness caused by mutations in the mitochondrial DNA (A) account for less than 1 percent of cases. These are inherited by all sons and daughters from mothers but not fathers.

109. D: Typical speech-language symptoms of Fragile X syndrome include self-talk (A) or talking to oneself using varying pitches and tones; perseveration (B)—not only repeating the same phrase over and over but also continually talking about the same subject; and cluttered speech (C), that is, lack of intelligibility due to lack of language organization, lack of relevance of the content, unclear articulation, too fast or irregular speech rates, running words together, and so on.

110. C: Turner syndrome is a chromosomal syndrome wherein a female has a missing or incomplete X chromosome. It can cause hearing and cognitive deficits. Hurler syndrome (A), Hunter syndrome (B), and phenylketonuria (D), which can cause speech or language problems, are all genetic syndromes that are classified as metabolic disorders rather than as chromosomal syndromes.

111. B: According to Principle of Ethics I, Rule J, SLPs can make reasonable statements of prognosis but will NOT directly state or imply a guarantee of results from any treatment or procedure they might provide. This does not mean they should say a prognosis is impossible because the SLP field is too complicated (A); or equate reasonable statements of prognosis with a guarantee (C), which they are not; or confine prognosis statements to standardized test results (D).

112. A: According to the ASHA Code of Ethics, Principle of Ethics III, Rule C, SLPs will only refer clients they have served based on the interest of the client and not based on "any personal interest (C), financial (B) or otherwise." Principle of Ethics IV, Rule J, states that SLPs will not render professional services "without exercising independent professional judgment, regardless of referral source or prescription" (D).

113. B: Principle of Ethics IV, Rule B of the ASHA Code of Ethics states that SLPs "shall prohibit anyone under their supervision from engaging in any practice that violates the Code of Ethics." Therefore, this is NOT the responsibility of the supervisee (A) but of the supervisor. Principle of Ethics I, Rule F states that SLPs with ASHA's CCC may delegate clinical, service-provision-related tasks to others "only if those services are appropriately supervised, realizing that the responsibility for client welfare remains with the certified individual." Therefore, the supervisor and NOT the delegated staff are responsible for client welfare (C). Principle of Ethics I, Rule E states that SLPs with the CCC will NOT delegate tasks requiring professional "skills, knowledge, and judgment" to any nonprofessionals they supervise (D).

114. C: A criterion-referenced test is more appropriate for this client than a norm-referenced test. Norm-referenced tests determine how the individual performs compared to the average. It is not clinically useful to compare the speech and language of an individual with severe aphasia to that of a normative group. It is more helpful to compare the client's performance to an expected performance level (in this case, to a clinical expectation of functional and intelligible speech and language) as criterion-referenced tests do. Unlike norm-referenced tests, which by definition are standardized, criterion-referenced tests may or may not be standardized. Both have advantages and disadvantages (e.g., there is some room for individualization with nonstandardized tests, whereas standardized ones are better known to facilitate consultations, more accepted by insurance providers for reimbursement and school districts for service eligibility, generally more objective, and more efficient to administer). Therefore, while the best choice is a criterion-referenced test, the SLP may choose either a standardized or nonstandardized one.

115. D: Internal consistency is the measure of reliability that estimates how similar all the items on one test are, that is, how well they correlate with each other. This measure is used often with norm-referenced tests. Test-retest reliability (A) measures how similar the results of a test will be when its administration to the same examinees is repeated after a short time. This shows how much a test can produce consistent scores. Parallel forms reliability (B) measures how similar multiple, parallel forms of a test are to one another. (Many standardized tests are designed with a Form A, Form B, and so on.) This measure estimates how consistent you can expect the same examinees' scores to be across the test forms. Decision consistency reliability (C) is often used with criterion-referenced tests that classify results as pass–fail rather than giving numerical scores or scaled ratings. If the same examinee either passes or fails in two separate administrations, the test yields consistent decisions. (This method can apply to parallel-forms or test-retest administrations.)

116. A: The factorial design is a complex experimental research design. It is used to study the effects of two or more independent variables (rather than just one) on the same dependent variable. The within-subjects design (A) compares the effects of all experimental treatment conditions applied to all participants. The pretest-posttest design (B) compares participant groups before and after experimental treatment conditions are applied. The between-subjects design (C) compares treatment groups to control groups of participants. These are all simple experimental research designs rather than complex designs.

117. B: The manual for any standardized test should be comprehensive and should include the rationale for the test (A); the qualifications needed for examiners to administer the test (B); a description of how the test was developed (C); and detailed instructions for administering, scoring, and interpreting the test (D), as well as indices of reliability and validity; information about the normative sample; and descriptive statistics, supplemented by visual graphs and informational tables to help examiners understand analysis procedures and more easily interpret the test results.

118. D: The National Center on Educational Outcomes (NCEO) has been tracking and analyzing the policies and practices of state education agencies regarding accommodations for students with disabilities to participate in statewide and district-wide testing, as mandated by the IDEA, since 1992. The NCEO reports that there is significant variation in the decisions about selecting and applying accommodations, not only among the states (B) and even within states (C), but even among individual schools (D). While the IDEA is a federal law, the ways that the states, districts, and schools interpret it differ; hence, these accommodation decisions are NOT uniform across the states (A).